Stylish Sewing

TECHNIQUES FOR
QUILTED AND EMBELLISHED
CLOTHING

Patricia Nelson

Martingale
& C O M P A N Y

Bothell, Washington

Credits

President . . . . Nancy J. Martin
CEO . . . . Daniel J. Martin
Publisher . . . . Jane Hamada
Editorial Director . . . . Mary V. Green
Technical Editor . . . . Laurie Baker
Copy Editor . . . . Ellen Balstad
Design and Production Manager . . . . Stan Green
Illustrators . . . . Laurel Strand, Jil Johänson
Photographer . . . . Brent Kane
Text Designer . . . . Rohani Design
Cover Designer . . . . Stan Green

That Patchwork Place is an imprint of
Martingale & Company.

Mission Statement

We are dedicated to providing quality products
and service by working together to inspire creativity
and to enrich the lives we touch.

Stylish Sewing: Techniques for Quilted and
Embellished Clothing
© 2000 by Patricia Nelson

Martingale & Company
PO Box 118
Bothell, WA 98041-0118 USA
www.patchwork.com

Printed in the United States
05 04 03 02 01 00   6 5 4 3 2 1

Library of Congress Cataloging-in-Publication Data

Nelson, Patricia.
    Stylish sewing : techniques for quilted and embellished clothing / Patricia Nelson.
        p. cm.
    ISBN 1-56477-299-3
        1. Clothing and dress. 2. Decoration and ornament.
    3. Fancy work. 4. Quilting. I. Title.
TT560 .N45 2000
746.46'0432—dc21   00-026006

Dedication

I would like to dedicate this book to the following people:
My husband, David, who has supported and encouraged
me to succeed all these years in my third career; my daughter, Krista, who is my color and design guru; and Jeanne
Novak and Deb Johnson, who were always there to advise
me through my indecision.

Contents

Introduction

Stylish Sewing is about elegant, practical, everyday wearable art that anyone can create and wear. It is a compilation of all the bits and pieces of knowledge I have gained over the years through workshops, books, and experience from my own mistakes. With *Stylish Sewing*, I hope to encourage you to view quilted clothing in a different light and to start making unique garments. I also hope to stimulate your mind through pictures and ideas, and the techniques that go with the ideas. *Stylish Sewing* acts as both a visual stimulant and as a technique guide to help create one-of-a-kind wearable garments.

Some of the features of the book include photos of my prize-winning garments and instructions on how to duplicate each technique. Learn how to mix techniques, textures, and embellishments to suit your individual style. Make clothing that is flattering, practical, and very wearable, and at the same time sharpen your machine skills. Become more aware of how to achieve the look you want and use your newly learned skills. Information on how to use current machine-art techniques and the equipment and supplies available is also provided; and an abundance of tips and prob-

lem-solving ideas are included, making it easier to create the garments.

As a final encouragement to the hesitant sewer, I am a registered nurse who has sewn since I was a small child. In later years, I took sewing classes wherever and whenever I could. I have read, observed, and listened to my peers to become more knowledgeable in color and other phases of quilting, fitting, and sewing. I love to sew and want to share what I have learned over the years to make it easy for you to create your own "stylish sewing."

—*Patricia Nelson*

Winterblooms (page 49)

The Design Process

The process for designing a garment is not the same for everyone. What works for me may not necessarily work for you, but if you have never designed before, my process will give you a place to start.

The first thing I need to create unique wearables like the ones you see in this book is visual stimulation. For me, the stimulation can be anything, from an eye-catching fabric to a favorite color combination, an interesting ready-to-wear garment, or a commercial pattern. One of my favorite ways to find ideas and become stimulated is to people-watch—I look at the styles, color combinations, and types of fabrics other people are wearing.

After I see something inspiring, I start to put the ideas together in my mind. Designing or "seeing" a garment in my head can happen any place at any time, but the ideas flow more readily when it is quiet and I am not distracted. Some of my most productive moments are the times just after waking and before I get up, when I am in the shower, when I am on the treadmill, or while I'm driving. (I live in a rural area with little traffic, and designing helps pass the time). To remember my ideas I use these three tools:

- A small sketchbook that fits nicely in my purse. This is essential for jotting down notes and making sketches when I am shopping or people watching.
- A photocopy of the pattern-piece schematics from the pattern guidesheet. These are especially helpful when planning design placement after selecting a pattern. You can test the design before you make your final pattern selection. They

Design Inspiration

The key to finding ideas is to keep your eyes open all the time and let your mind wander! Here are some other things that have inspired me to create new designs:

- New techniques
- Fabulous patterns that look great on my body shape
- Nature, such as falling leaves, snow, birds, and flowers in bloom
- Ready-to-wear garments
- Pictures in magazines
- A museum exhibit
- Floor tile
- Specialty threads and yarns
- A great pair of slacks that needed a vest or jacket
- Television fashion shows

are also good just for doodling ideas. For general purposes, enlarge the front, back, and sleeve pieces from the schematic of a favorite vest, jacket, blouse, pant, or skirt pattern. Make several photocopies so that you can record your design ideas.
- A hand-held tape recorder. This device is a must-have for using in the car when an idea strikes but you can't or don't have time to sketch it out.

Mental Exercise

If you're having trouble designing your garment, answering the following questions will help you think about the look you want to achieve in the finished garment.

What is your focus? Do you want to make a jacket, a coat, a vest, or a complete ensemble?

What will be the use or purpose of the finished garment? Will it be casual, sporty, formal, or informal? What season of the year will it be used?

What will be the theme or design of the garment? Do you want a garment that reminds you of spring flowers, the winds of winter, or perhaps just a great garment that has a geometric theme or textures?

What technique do you want to use? There are numerous techniques that can be used individually or together. Determine what technique works best for your fabric, pattern, and design. Be sure to take your skill level into consideration, too.

Do you want the garment to be subtle or bold? Do you want to use one or more colors? Are the colors flattering to you?

What pattern do you want to use? Will the pattern lines accommodate your design ideas? Are the pattern lines flattering to your body shape? (Refer to "Patterns" on page 9 for more information.)

What fabric(s) do you want to use? Is the fabric appropriate for the time of year the garment will be used? Will the fabric work with the designs you have in mind? Is the fabric appropriate for the pattern? Is the fabric flattering to your coloring and body shape or size?

I have also been known to whip out the checkbook and doodle on the back of deposit slips. Sometimes ideas lay dormant for a year before I act upon them, but as long as I have the basic idea written down it is easy to embellish and elaborate on a theme at a later time.

After the design is conceived, I choose a pattern, fabric, thread, and trim that seem to fit the design, are complementary to my coloring and body shape, work with the techniques I plan to use, and are appropriate for the situation where I plan to wear the garment. Sometimes I work in reverse and buy a special fabric and wait for the right technique or design to come to mind.

When I have melded ideas, fabrics, and techniques together, I start making samples to see if all the components work together. I strongly recommend making samples. They save time, tears, and frustration!

Black and Tan (page 59)

Getting Ready

Inspiration is key to creating wonderful quilted and embellished garments, but that is not all you need. Having the right tools and some basic sewing knowledge helps make the experience much more enjoyable and successful. This first chapter covers the basic materials and tools used to make the projects presented. Each of the individual projects list specific techniques and materials needed to make the garment.

PATTERNS

With a background in nursing, designing a pattern from scratch is not my forte, so I use commercial patterns as the base for my designs and alter them as needed to fit. Because the techniques presented in this book can be used on many styles of garments, I do not specify a particular pattern, but I do recommend a suitable style of pattern.

Choosing a Flattering Style

The first step to selecting a pattern is to decide what style of clothing is flattering to your body. The easiest way to determine this is to go to a store and try on different styles of clothes to find what is suitable for you. Ask a friend who will give you an honest opinion to go with you, and take a tape measure so that you can determine specifics, such as finished jacket and vest back length and skirt and pant length and width, that are flattering to your body. You may find several lengths flattering, so don't stop at just one! Personally, I have three vest/ jacket lengths that are best for me: a shorter length for wearing with skirts and two longer lengths for slacks.

Once you've found some flattering styles, look at the current pattern books and select patterns with styles similar to the clothing you liked at the store. I have found that a pattern with princess seams or bust darts is flattering to many body types and is easier to fit on women with busts larger than a B cup. This style is also great when using heavily textured and quilted fabrics.

Selecting the Right Size

It is imperative to a good fit to use the correct pattern size. Knowing how to purchase the correct pattern size minimizes alterations. First of all, do not automatically purchase a pattern in the same size you would wear in ready-to-wear clothing. Purchase the pattern based on your measurements. In most cases, your pattern size will be larger than the size you wear in ready-to-wear clothing. This is normal. For example, I wear a size 10 when purchasing off the rack but use a size 14 pattern when making vests, blouses, jackets, and coats, and size 14 or 16 when sewing skirts and pants.

The following information will help you determine the correct pattern size to purchase when making *fitted* garments. Looser-style garments have more room in them due to the garment design, so exact fitting is not as critical. For books with in-depth information on fitting, see "Bibliography" on page 111.

For tops, vests, and jackets, take your high bust measurement, as well as your bust measurement, to determine the pattern size required for a good upper-body fit. Measure the high bust by bringing the tape measure across the widest part of the back, high under the arms, and *above* the fullest part of the bust. Take the bust measurement by bringing the tape measure across the widest part of the back, under the arms, and *over* the fullest part of the bust. Keep the tape measure parallel with the ground.

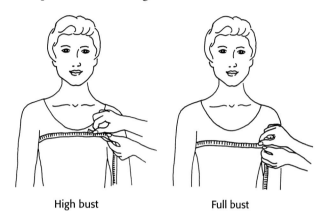

High bust   Full bust

If the difference between the two measurements is less than 2", purchase the pattern according to your bust measurement. If the difference between the two measurements is more than 2", purchase the pattern according to your high-bust measurement (this is what most people with cup sizes larger than B do). This will help achieve a better fit in the shoulder and upper-chest area but may require some small alterations in the bust area. Alterations in the bust area are easier to do than the upper chest and shoulder areas.

For further verification of your size, add the appropriate amount of wearing ease (the amount of inches you need to add to the garment for the body to move without being constricted or uncomfortable) to your bust measurement; then compare this measurement with the *finished* bust measurement of the garment listed on either the outside of the pattern envelope or on the front bodice piece. Use the chart at right to determine the minimum ease required, then select the size that is closest to your bust measurement with the ease added. For example, if your bust measures 38", add 3" for ease for a total of 41". This is the amount of room needed for a vest or blouse to fit around your body and give you room to move.

If you are between sizes, determining your

type of bone structure may help you decide your size. A person with a small bone structure or frame would likely go to the lower size, while a person with a larger frame should go up to the next size. Personal fitting preference can also determine size. If you like your clothes looser, go up to the next size, and vice versa if you like your clothes more fitted.

For pants or skirts, purchase patterns according to your hip measurement. Measure your hip around the fullest part, which is usually 6" to 9" below your waistline. Check the pattern measurements and compare your hip size, with ease added, to ensure a good fit.

Minimum Ease for Fitted Garments

Bust	
Blouse or dress	2½" to 3"
Vest or jacket	3" to 5"
Coat	4" to 6"
Waist	1" to 1½"
Hip	2" to 3"

FASHION FABRICS

I find fashion fabrics (the ones used for the right side of the garment) in all kinds of places: stores, catalogs, magazine ads in sewing magazines, and even garage sales. Follow the manufacturer's instructions to pretreat the fabrics as necessary or as desired for the final finished look. Some wools need to be dry-cleaned before use (check the bolt end) and others are ready for use. Silks can be hand washed, but be aware that darker colors tend to bleed and should be dry-cleaned for that reason. Cottons can be prewashed or not, depending on the desired finished look. When I machine quilt and trapunto a cotton garment, I usually do not prewash the fabric so that it gets a wonderful puckered look after it is washed and dried. Trapunto, which is a decorative quilted design in high relief worked through at least two layers of cloth, is described in greater detail on page 39.

described in greater detail on page 39.

Tip Starch very slippery fabrics so that they behave during cutting and sewing. Dilute liquid starch with an equal amount of tap water. Soak the fabric in the solution and allow it to air-dry. Press it; then cut out the pieces. Wash the starch out when the garment is finished.

How do I know which fabrics to use and where? Experimenting with different fabric weights, interfacings, battings, and backing fabrics is the best teacher when trying out new techniques. Purchase a quarter yard of a questionable fabric and do technique samples. It may seem like a nuisance, but it pays off. Many seemingly unsuitable lightweight fabrics are perfect when quilted.

After you make your technique samples but before you cut into your fashion fabric, if you are using a new pattern, make a mock-up of your garment with unwanted or leftover fabric. I use either lightweight denim, gabardine, or corduroy left over from the days when I sewed clothing for my small children. I have found that muslin does not give me an accurate idea for how a quilted or heavily textured vest, coat, or jacket is going to hang when it is finished.

INTERFACINGS

I use fusible interfacing in my garments to stabilize the fabric before working with it, as well as to reinforce items such as facings and collars. Use a tricot interfacing when a softer drape is desired and a woven interfacing when a firmer finish is needed. Woven interfacings most often come in widths of 22". Therefore, a mock layout of the pattern pieces is necessary to calculate interfacing yardage. This 22"-width may also present a problem when stabilizing a garment back. If the interfacing is wide enough, fold it in half and place the center back line of the pattern on the fold line. If the interfacing is not wide enough to cut out the back on the center fold, place the back pattern piece on two layers of interfacing, resin sides together. Cut out the interfacing, adding ½" along the center back line; draw the center back line on the interfacing pieces with a pencil. Overlap the pieces ½", lining up the pencil lines, and place the resin sides down. Stitch the pieces together on the pencil line. Trim the seam allowance to ¼". When doing mock layouts, be sure to add enough yardage to cut two back pieces.

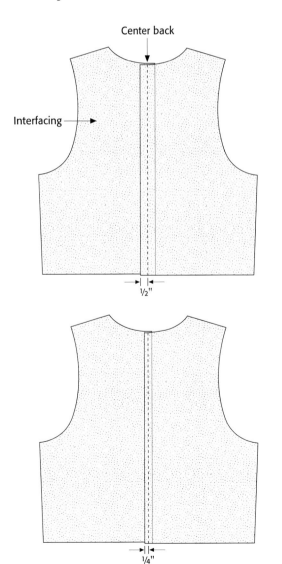

Prewash fusible interfacing before using it. To do so, loosely fold the interfacing and immerse it in a sink filled with hot tap water. Let it sit unagitated until the water is cool. Drain the water and let the interfacing remain in the sink until there is no water dripping from it. Hang woven interfacing over a rod to air-dry; lay tricot interfacing flat to dry. If time is of the essence, roll up the interfacing in a towel to remove the excess water; then air-dry it.

 Purchase a spring-tension curtain rod to fit over the bathtub. It makes drying the interfacing easier because all the drips will be in the tub.

Fusible interfacing requires three things to be most effective: heat, steam, and pressure. You will also have better results if you press the interfaced piece from the fabric right side after you have fused it to the fabric wrong side. Check the instructions that come with the interfacing for the recommended pressing time and iron setting. Fabrics that won't tolerate higher temperatures can be fused using lower temperatures, but a longer pressing time is required.

 If bubbling occurs on the interfacing, and you have prewashed it, it could mean that either the fabric has shrunk or the iron is too hot. Try reducing the iron temperature first. If you still have problems, prewash or dry-clean the fabric.

 Cut leftover interfacing scraps into 2"-wide strips to use later for stabilizing neck and button-hole areas.

FUSIBLE WEBBING

I use regular-weight, paper-backed fusible webbing to hold appliqués in place before permanently stitching them to garments. Follow the manufacturer's instructions for the recommended fusing technique and keep the web rolled up when it is not in use.

SEWING MACHINE

A top-of-the-line sewing machine with embroidery capabilities is a wonderful piece of machinery to own for fashioning wearable works of art, but it is not necessary for most of the techniques presented in this book. If you have a basic machine that will do a zigzag stitch, you will be well on your way to creating a fabulous wardrobe. For those garments that do feature embellishments created with built-in embroidery stitches, get creative and substitute these stitches with your own unique idea.

When machine quilting, you will need a sewing machine with feed dogs that can be lowered or covered, as well as a darning foot and/or walking foot. An extension plate for your sewing machine is also helpful. If your machine does not have an extension plate, check with your sewing machine dealer or a sewing notions mail-order catalog about ordering a custom-cut Plexiglas plate to fit your machine. The extended area makes sewing with large pieces much easier.

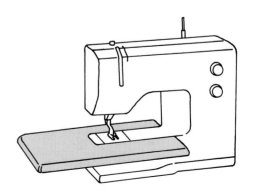

Understanding Tension

All sewers need to understand how to achieve a balanced tension on their sewing machine before they construct a garment. Once you understand this, you will be able to work effectively with a variety of threads to create decorative effects.

A balanced tension is necessary to sew strong seams when constructing a garment. To check for balanced tension, thread the needle and bobbin with different colors of the same weight of thread, and set the machine for 10 to 12 stitches per inch. Fold a piece of scrap fabric in half to create two layers; then stitch across it. If your tension is balanced, the upper and lower threads will lock between the fabric layers.

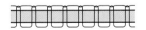

Balanced tension

If you can see little dots of bobbin thread between the stitches on the right side of the fabric, the top tension is too tight. Loosen the tension control half a number and test again. If necessary, continue to adjust the tension half a number at a time until the bobbin thread no longer shows.

NOTE: USING A NEEDLE SIZE THAT IS TOO LARGE FOR THE FABRIC WEIGHT CAN ALSO CAUSE UNBALANCED TENSION.

Top tension too tight

Turn your sample over and look at the reverse side of your row of stitches. If you can see little dots of the top thread showing through, the top tension is too loose. Tighten the tension control in half-number increments until a balanced top tension is achieved.

Top tension too loose

Bobbin tension can be adjusted to achieve different decorative effects by adjusting the screw on the side of the bobbin case. However, if you have a machine with a removable bobbin case, I strongly recommend obtaining a second bobbin case to use for this purpose so that you can easily return to the tension needed for constructing the garment. Paint the bobbin latch with a dot of fingernail polish to distinguish it from your bobbin case for regular sewing.

To tighten the bobbin tension, turn the screw with a screwdriver to the right; to loosen, turn the screw to the left. Remember, "Righty tighty, lefty loosey."

Right to tighten   Left to loosen

Bobbin Tension Adjustment

To tell if you have balanced tension, thread the bobbin case as usual with a full bobbin. Hold the thread end in the air with the bobbin case dangling. If the bobbin case falls, then the tension is too loose. Tighten it and hold the case by the bobbin thread again to see if it falls. Repeat this step until the only way the thread unwinds is if you bounce the bobbin case slightly, as if it were a yo-yo. The tension is too tight if you are not able to bounce thread from the bobbin case.

Tip

To keep from losing the screw when you are adjusting the bobbin case, place the bobbin case in a clear plastic bag and adjust the screw inside the bag. If the screw and spring pop out, you won't lose the pieces, and you can take the case to your sewing machine dealer and have him put it back together for you.

Machine Setup and Stitching Techniques

The stitching techniques presented throughout this book use one of the following two machine setups: regular/machine-guided or free-motion.

Regular or Machine-Guided

Regular or machine-guided stitching means that the sewing machine, with the aid of the machine's feed dogs, does the work of moving the fabric layers evenly under the needle. The feed dogs are up, and the stitch length, width, and tension are set for a balanced stitch. When constructing a garment, attach the all-purpose or zigzag foot to the machine, depending on the stitch desired. When stitching multiple layers together, such as when you machine quilt, use a walking foot. Stitching with the walking foot, however, is limited to straight rows, like those used for channel quilting, crosshatch, and gently curving lines (see "Quilting Designs" on page 28).

Free-Motion

Free-motion stitching lets *you* control the direction that the fabric layers are moved. Because the feed dogs are dropped, you have the freedom to move in any direction. This ability allows you to create virtually any design or even follow the design of a printed fabric.

To set your machine up for free-motion stitching, attach a darning foot, drop or cover the feed dogs (refer to your sewing machine manual), and set the stitch length and width at 0. Stitch length is determined by how fast you move the fabric layers under the needle. As easy as that sounds, creating equally spaced stitches takes practice; you must move the layers and the machine at consistent rates of speed. If you move the fabric slower than the needle speed, your stitches will be very short. If you move the fabric faster than the needle speed, your stitches will be too long. Try holding the fabric layers one of the following ways to find a method you are comfortable with and that helps you achieve the most even stitch length.

- Hold the edges of the piece you are stitching on either side of the presser foot.

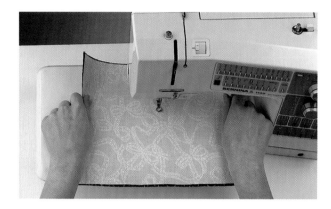

- Hold one edge of the piece you are stitching and lay your other hand flat on the opposite side of the presser foot.

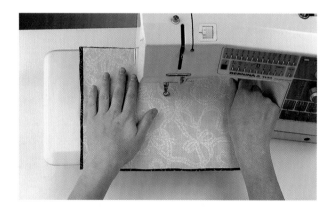

- Place both hands flat on either side of the presser foot.

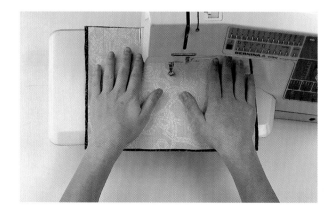

Machine Setup Hints

- Make sure the presser foot and the thread take-up lever are in the up position when threading or you will find a big tangled mess on the bottom of your work when starting to sew. Believe me, there is nothing worse to try and untangle!
- Always bring the bobbin thread up to the top of your work and hold both threads before starting to sew.
- Anytime you are stitching with the feed dogs lowered, remember to lower your presser foot lever to avoid thread jams as you begin sewing.

 Tip For those who have trouble threading the needle, cut the thread at an angle, hold the thread between your forefingers, and aim for the needle's eye. You can also try holding a piece of white paper behind the needle to help illuminate the eye of the needle.

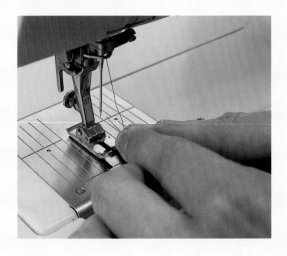

Cleaning Your Machine

Your sewing machine needs to be kept clean to run efficiently. Check your sewing machine manual for directions on how to maintain your machine or ask the service technician at the dealership where you purchased the machine.

 Tip Never blow lint out of your machine with your mouth; the lint can pack further into your machine, plus the moisture from your breath can start a rusting reaction.

NEEDLES

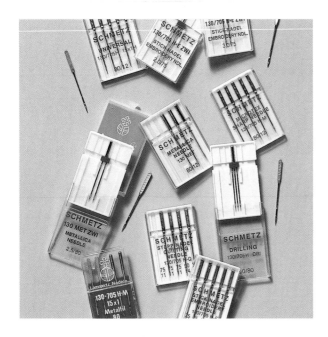

Years ago sewing was primarily a utilitarian task, and there was not much need for different kinds of needles. Today, however, sewers employ their machines to do creative stitching with a variety of threads, and often a regular sharp- or ball-point needle does not produce satisfactory results. Thankfully, needle manufacturers have responded to the requests of sewers and now offer needles made specifically for working with these variables.

Picking the Correct Type and Size

With all the different needles available, how do you select the right one? The first thing to consider is the fabric you will use to construct your garment. Select the type of needle based on the fabric structure. Sharp-point needles are recommended for woven fabrics, while ball-point needles should be used for all knit and stretch fabrics. Universal needles can be used with both woven and knit fabrics and are what I call for in the materials section for constructing the projects in this book. While I find that a universal needle produces satisfactory results for most of my pro-

jects, the fabrics and threads you are using may require a different type. Be sure to make samples and adjust the needle type if necessary.

Next, pick the needle size appropriate for the fabric weight. Needle sizes are written on the case as well as the needle shank. You will notice two numbers: the first is the European size, the second is the American size. In general, the rule is: the finer the fabric, the finer the needle. For example, a needle marked 60/8 (the finest) is intended for use with lightweight fabrics, while a 120/20 (the coarsest) would be used for heavyweight fabrics.

Thread type and size also play a large part in needle selection. If the eye of the needle is too small for the thread(s), the thread shreds; if the needle is too large, you see holes along the seam where the thread was unable to fill the hole created by the needle.

Tip — Remember the thread rule: the eye of the needle should be twice the size of the thread. Many of the newer needle types have been created for use with specialty threads. Look for needles specifically designed for sewing with metallic, topstitching, and embroidery threads.

Sewing with Twin and Triple Needles

Many special effects, like topstitching, pintucking, and machine quilting, also can be created with twin and triple needles. These needles are sized with the first number being the amount of space between the needles and the second number being the European size of the needle. For example, a twin needle sized 2.5/80 means that the needles are 2.5 millimeters apart and a size 80 European (12 American).

When using and threading twin needles, determine if the thread spools must be on side-by-side spindles. If they must, place the spools so that they unwind in opposite directions to

Needle Size Conversion Chart

European	60	65	70	75	80	90	100	110	120
American	8	9	10	11	12	14	16	18	20

prevent them from rubbing against each other. Place the threads on opposite sides of the tension discs, if possible. Insert the thread from the right spool on the right side of the discs into the right needle and the thread from the left spool on the left side of the discs into the left needle. For triple needles, place one spool of thread on a thread stand and the other two spools in the same manner as you would for a twin needle. Place two of the threads on one side of the tension discs, and the remaining thread on the other side. If the threads twist and break while sewing, thread only one thread through the last thread guide, leaving the other threads outside the guide.

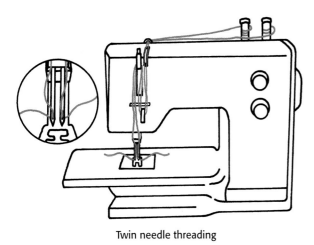

Twin needle threading

If your machine has a twin-needle function button, use it whenever you plan on using multiple needles with any stitch other than a straight stitch. This helps prevent the needles from swinging wider than the width possible for your machine, avoiding needle breakage and possible damage to your machine and fabrics.

To create different effects with twin and triple needles, adjust the tension. For example, to achieve a double row of flat stitches, loosen the tension. For raised pintucks, tighten the tension.

THREADS

The variety of threads, like needles, has enjoyed a huge explosion in the past few years. In this section, I discuss the ones used throughout this book.

All-Purpose

This is the thread that holds your project together, so buy good-quality threads; bargain threads only disappoint and frustrate you by breaking and building up lint. Use 100 percent cotton, 100 percent polyester, or a cotton-and-polyester blend that is compatible with the fabric you are sewing.

Rayon

These beautiful, shiny threads are wonderful for machine embroidery, machine quilting, and topstitching. The most common rayon thread weights available are 30 and 40, with 30 being the heaviest. Both weights are available in a variety of colors. A twisted variety, consisting of two thinner-weight rayon threads, is available in 35 weight.

A single or twin embroidery needle works well with these threads for most techniques; however, if you stitch with two threads and one needle, use a topstitching size 80/12 needle because it has an eye large enough to accommodate the extra thread. Follow the threading technique for stitching with a twin needle.

Because they are slippery, some rayon threads have a tendency to fall off their spool when they are in a vertical position, causing the thread to wind around the spindle and break. There are several solutions to this problem, including the following suggestions:

- If a horizontal spindle is available for your machine, use it.
- If your machine has a thread hook on the back side of the carrying handle, raise the handle and insert the thread through the eye. Continue threading the machine as normal.

- Position the spool in a container that has been placed under the spindles behind the machine. Place a safety pin on the thread spindle. When threading, bring the thread up from the container and pass it through the loop of the safety pin. Continue threading the machine as normal.

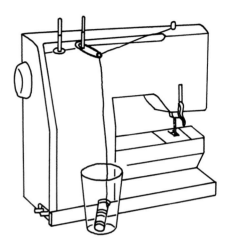

- Use a thread stand.

If you are heavily stitching an area with rayon thread, such as in machine embroidering, use bobbin thread (see page 20) in the bobbin to lessen thread buildup on the wrong side of the fabric.

Metallic

These glistening gems add sparkle to machine quilting, embroidery, and topstitching, but they often present a great stitching challenge. To avoid problems, consider the needle, tension, and bobbin thread when working with metallic thread. Use a needle made specifically for metallic thread. If you cannot find one, I have found that a topstitching needle, size 90/14, works well. Loosen the top tension when working with these fragile threads. The amount to loosen will depend on your machine, the bobbin thread, and the humidity. I have found that the more humid it is, the more my thread breaks if I don't loosen the top tension sufficiently. All-purpose thread generally works in the bobbin, but if you are having breakage problems, try using bobbin thread. Bobbin thread (see page 20) is finer and allows the tension to be lowered enough to prevent thread breakage and to achieve balanced stitch tension.

 Use a vertical spool spindle when sewing with metallic threads. If you do not have a vertical spindle, special attachments are available to convert a horizontal spindle to a vertical one. Check with your sewing-machine dealer.

If you are still having problems working with metallic thread, a silicone thread lubricant, such as Sewer's Aid, may help. There are many methods for applying the lubricant, but I like the following method that my machine technician recommended: saturate one end of two cotton swabs with lubricant. Cross the lubricated ends in an X shape, and tape them to the machine just above the tension discs. Position the thread between the swabs.

NOTE: A SILICONE LUBRICANT MAY HARM SOME MACHINES. BE SURE TO CHECK WITH YOUR SEWING MACHINE DEALER BEFORE USING ONE.

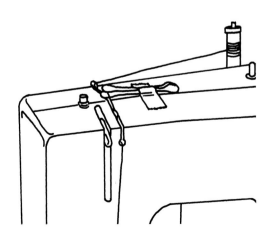

Quilting

There are several quilting threads on the market suitable for machine sewing. Look for quilting thread that does not have any coating or wax substance on it. I use them in projects for top-stitching the finished edge of garments and for decorative embellishing. For best results when using quilting thread, use a topstitching needle; in the bobbin, use either quilting thread or all-purpose thread.

Invisible Monofilament

Invisible monofilament thread is used for outlining motifs and appliqués, dense quilting on garments with batting, attaching braids and trims, and for any decorative applications where you don't want the thread to be seen. It is available in clear and smoke and is especially useful if you are working with more than one color in the garment and do not want to continually change thread colors to keep the thread from being noticeable. Use it in the bobbin and needle if a reversible garment is desired.

Many quilters do not like invisible thread because they think it will cut the fabric or their sewing thread because it is stronger. Using .004 millimeter thread, as well as a balanced tension, prevents this from happening. Since seeing is believing, try this test. Cut 18" lengths of .004-millimeter invisible thread and 50/3 (size 50, 3-ply) all-purpose cotton thread. Holding both threads in one hand, wrap them around your fist, then pick up the other two ends and wrap them around your other fist. Proceed to stretch them until you break them. The threads will break at approximately the same time, which indicates that they are close to the same strength and one will not cut the other.

To test for a balanced tension when you are using invisible thread in both the bobbin and needle, stitch a row of straight stitches for approximately 2". Pull the top thread out. If there is no resistance when you pull it out, the top tension is too tight. Loosen it by half of a number and repeat the first step. Keep running rows of stitches and loosening the tension until there is some resistance to pulling out the top thread. Once you are satisfied with the top tension, run another row of stitches to check the bobbin tension. If there is no resistance and the bobbin thread pulls out very easily, the top tension has been loosened too much. Tighten the top tension gradually until the resistance on the bobbin thread is about the same as on the top thread. This may seem tedious, but it usually only takes a couple of tries to balance the tension this way. When it is balanced, both threads should pull out with the same resistance. Make a note of the settings that worked for you. This technique works best with a needle size compatible with the fabric and invisible thread (needle size 11 or 12).

Bobbin

For most of the decorative threadwork in this book, you will need to use a finer thread in the bobbin than in the needle. There are several options available. Bobbin thread, often referred to as lingerie thread, is very fine and slightly stretchy. Because it is so fine, it is the perfect choice for machine embroidering because it lessens the thread buildup on the wrong side of the fabric. It is also helpful to use bobbin thread if you are having tension problems when using metallic thread in the needle. Bobbin thread is available in white and black.

Cotton embroidery thread and polyester/cotton-blend threads also come in the finer weight, size 60, needed for use in the bobbin, and they are available in many colors. This makes them ideal for reversible work.

SCISSORS

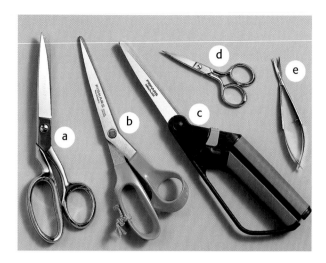

Sharp scissors are a must. The scissors I use most are 8" knife-edge, bent-handle dressmaker's shears for trimming seams (a); 4" and 8" paper scissors (b); 8" bent-handle, spring action dressmaker's shears for cutting fabric (c); 4" embroidery scissors for trimming in tight areas (d); and 4½" curved tip, squeeze snips for clipping threads (e).

PINS

You will want to make sure that you have plenty of .50-millimeter, glass-head straight pins for pin-basting quilt "sandwiches" and pinning garment pieces together.

MARKING TOOLS

Marking tools are very important for transferring designs. Because there are so many different marking tools available, it is essential to test each one for ease of removal before using it on a fabric.

Machine work requires a very clear line to sew on, so use a water-soluble marker to trace designs onto light fabrics and a light-color chalk pencil for marking on dark fabrics. Follow the manufacturer's directions for transferring and removing the markings.

Other marking tools I have used for projects include fine-line, permanent-ink pens, pencils, and a chalk wheel. Wax-free transfer paper and tracing paper are also very handy for transferring larger designs.

Always test the marking tool on a scrap of fabric before using it on your garment to be sure the marks can be removed.

PRESSING EQUIPMENT

Steam, pressure, and drying time are necessary to achieve a professional finished look in garments. The following items are some tools that will help your garments look their best.

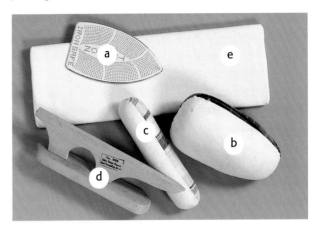

For all seams, unless otherwise indicated, press them flat first to relax the stitches, then press them open.

- The Iron Safe (a) is a Teflon-coated plate that clips onto the iron sole plate and allows you to use high levels of steam and heat without damaging delicate fabrics. The coating also keeps fusible webs from sticking to the plate.
- Use a tailor's ham (b) for pressing shaped areas such as darts and curved seams.
- Press seams open over a seam roll (c) to prevent seam-allowance impressions on the right side of the fabric.
- Use a wooden point presser and clapper (d) to flatten seams after steaming them, and to obtain a crisp look when pressing facings, collars, and lapels. After steaming, do not move the garment until it is dry. Handling the garment before it is dry could result in stretching, especially if it is wool.

- A pants seam board (e) is a homemade tool that allows you to press pants seams made from fabrics that don't need to be steamed. To make your own, cover an empty cardboard fabric bolt with muslin. To use, just slip it into a pant leg after the seams are sewn to press them open.

 Wools and some other fabrics need to be steamed rather than pressed to prevent shine and seam lines from showing through to the right side of the garment. Place the garment on the ironing board and gently finger-press the seams open. Hold the iron about ½" to 1" over the seam and press the iron's steam button. Immediately place a wooden clapper on the seam until it is cool. Continue in this manner to steam the entire seam. Do not move the freshly pressed fabric until it is dry.

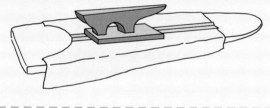

Stylized Flowers Vest
(page 99)

 If you have trouble getting a really flat seam on your wool garments, send them to a dry cleaner to be pressed. A dry cleaner is able to generate more steam to flatten seams so the garment looks professionally finished. Be sure to tell the dry cleaner that you do not want any seam lines showing through to the right side of the garment.

PROJECT WORKSHEET

The project worksheet on page 24 is invaluable for keeping track of expenses and the specific materials used. It is especially nice to have on hand when you are trying to duplicate the look of a previously made garment. Keep the worksheet in a plastic sheet protector along with a picture of the finished work and samples made during construction. File the sheets in a binder.

Senior Prom (page 48)

Baby It's Cold Outside (page 50)

Project Worksheet

Project description or title: _____

Date started: _____   Date finished: _____

Pattern company and number:

Pattern size:

Batting size and type:

Thread type for:

- Piecing and construction:

- Quilting:

- Embellishments:

Fabrics and yardages:

Special instructions or alterations:

Swatches:

Expenses:

    Fashion fabric:

    Backing or lining fabrics:

    Batting:

    Thread:

    Embellishments:

    Buttons:

    Zippers:

    Pattern:

    Other:

Machine Quilting

Quilting is a familiar technique in which two or more layers are stitched together with padding between them. It has been done by hand for centuries, but with the advances in machine technology, coupled with the introduction of new threads and battings, machine quilting is becoming more and more popular.

Machine quilting can be performed using either a machine-guided setup or free-motion setup (see "Machine Setup and Stitching Techniques" on page 14). The method to use is generally dictated by the quilting design.

MATERIALS

Backing

Many types of fashion fabric can be machine quilted, but it is important to consider how all the layers—fashion fabric, batting, and backing—will react with each other. Backing fabric greatly affects the way a garment hangs. A loosely woven backing fabric tends to give the quilt "sandwich" a more flexible feel than a tightly woven fabric does. I have used single-knit cotton fabrics, polyester or rayon lining fabrics, very loosely woven fabrics, muslin, and quilting cottons as backing. Each backing gives a finished garment a different feel. To see how the backing affects each sample, make several quilted samples with the same fashion fabric and batting but a different backing fabric. Always be sure to purchase additional fabric for making samples and to provide you with enough room for cutting the pieces larger than the patterns.

Batting

Batting is a major factor in the outcome of your finished garment. The proper drape of your fabric "sandwich" will determine the success of your finished garment. You want your quilted garments to be soft and flexible to the touch. To make intelligent decisions about which batting to use, I make samples for every garment, with different types of battings and backings. The quilted samples should feel flexible and soft, not stiff. These samples are

essential for finding out which batting has the perfect feel for the garment I am creating. You must familiarize yourself with what is available on the market. There are many wonderful battings from which to choose, but try to use only name-brand battings. I have no particular favorites and use the one that fits my needs at the time.

I use two kinds of batting: bonded and needlepunched. Bonded battings are treated with heat or resin on both sides to prevent the fibers from migrating through the fashion fabric. Bonded battings pull apart easily; however, one half is usually thinner than the other is. I have successfully split several different bonded battings to get thinner batting. I generally quilt whole garments with a thinner batting and use the thicker battings for trapunto work.

Note: IF YOU USE SPLIT BATTING, PLACE THE RESIN SIDE FACING THE WRONG SIDE OF THE FASHION FABRIC.

Needlepunched battings, designated on the chart on page 27 by the letters *NP*, are run through a machine with barbed needles that twist and tangle the fibers together to prevent fiber migration. They cannot be split. If possible, avoid battings that have been needlepunched to a base (scrim) to make them more stable. They may make your garment stiffer than you want.

In addition to choosing between bonded and needlepunched battings, you must choose what you want your batting to be made from. I recommend 100 percent cotton, 80 percent cotton/20 percent polyester blends, and 100 percent polyester battings. Unwashed cotton and cotton/polyester battings paired with unwashed fabrics will produce a beautiful, old-fashioned puckered texture to a quilted garment after washing. Polyester battings paired with prewashed fabrics will give a smooth look to the quilting without the puckered texture.

The battings I use most are listed in the chart below, but there are many more available that are fine to use.

Depending on the type of batting, you will need to pin-baste the quilt "sandwich" every 2" to 4". Polyester battings require pin-basting at least every 2" and sometimes closer. Cotton battings can be pinned as far apart as 4". I use .50-millimeter straight pins for pinning the layers together.

 Store each type of batting in a clear plastic trash bag with the original packaging at the bottom of the bag.

 Take the batting for your project out of the bag and unfold it twenty-four hours before use.

Consider the following when choosing batting:

• Do you want the garment to be warm? Polyester battings retain heat because they don't breathe, but cotton does.
• Are you using light or dark fabrics? The fibers of any batting other than 100 percent cotton can migrate through the fabric, leaving unsightly fuzzies on the fashion fabric. This process is called bearding. If you are using bonded polyester batting, densely quilting the fabric helps

Polyester	*Cotton/Polyester Blends*	*Cotton*
THINNER BATTINGS		
Hobbs Thermore	Hobbs Heirloom Premium (NP)	Hobbs Heirloom Organic (NP)
Fairfield Low-Loft	Fairfield Cotton Classic	Fairfield Soft Touch (NP)
Mountain Mist Quilt-Light		Mountain Mist 100% Cotton
Mountain Mist Mini-Light & More		Mountain Mist Blue Ribbon
THICKER BATTINGS		
Hobbs Polydown and Polydown-DK		
Fairfield Extra Loft Fairfield Hi-Loft		
Mountain Mist Polyester Mountain Mist Fatt Batt		

eliminate bearding. For dark fabrics, you can use a dark-color batting like Hobbs Polydown-DK. With unbleached cotton battings there is a possibility of stains from leftover leaf and seed debris in the batting; this can be a problem with light fabrics but not with dark fabrics.

 When choosing a pattern for a quilted garment with sleeves, select one with set-in or raglan sleeves. Quilted garments with off-the-shoulder sleeves do not always drape well.

• How do you want the garment to drape? Thicker battings generally create a firmer, bulkier finished product. An exception is the vest from "Evening Tango" (page 49). The silk used in the vest is such a soft, pliable fabric that it quilted beautifully with a thicker batting. The best way to determine which batting is best for your project is to make samples before quilting.

 When making samples, always use the same stitch and threads you will use on the garment. Use the practice samples to check thread tension, make buttonholes, and try out different trims.

STARTING AND STOPPING STITCHING

When quilting, threads must be locked off when starting and stopping stitching, but backstitching is not adequate. If your machine has a lock-off stitch, use it when you start and stop stitching. If not, begin and end your stitching with a ¼" line of very short stitches. When you are using a walking foot, set the stitch length almost to the buttonhole stitch length on your sewing machine dial. If you are free-motion quilting, move the fabric very slowly to create the short stitches.

It is often undesirable to lock off stitches on a lined garment. If this is the case, leave long thread tails at the beginning and end of the stitching, pull them to the back of the piece, and knot them. Clip the thread ends ½" from the fabric. Apply seam sealant to the knot to keep it from raveling.

 If the bobbin thread runs out while you're stitching, pull the bobbin tail to the top and clip both threads close to the fabric. Start stitching about ¼" before the break, taking several tiny stitches over the previous stitching before returning to a normal stitch length.

QUILTING DESIGNS

There are many types of quilting designs that can be used for your quilted garment, from straight lines to intricate floral patterns. The space you are trying to fill and the effect you are trying to achieve will help you determine which one is right for your project.

Machine-Guided Quilting

These are the simplest of all the quilting designs to accomplish. Because the machine is feeding the fabric layers under the needle, the result is consistently spaced stitches. Just attach your walking foot, raise the feed dogs, set the stitch length, and stitch away. However, because the machine is feeding the fabric, you are limited to straight and gently curved lines. Some examples of machine-guided designs include channel quilting and cross-hatching.

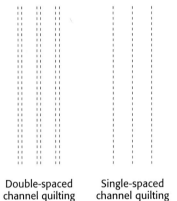

Double-spaced channel quilting   Single-spaced channel quilting

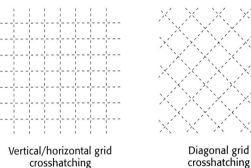

Vertical/horizontal grid crosshatching

Diagonal grid crosshatching

Free-Motion Quilting

Because the machine is set up for free-motion stitching and you are controlling the way the fabric is moved, virtually any design can fit into this category—even the ones listed in the machine-guided section. Some designs are based on specific patterns that are drawn onto the quilt top, while others are the epitome of free form and follow no specific lines.

Quilting designs that follow a specific pattern can be found in all sorts of places. In addition to finding them in books devoted to the subject, look for inspiration in fabrics, wallpaper, ceiling and floor tiles, buildings, and furniture. Dover Books has many copyright-free designs that work well for quilting when they are enlarged. Quilt history books also have very unusual designs.

Once you find a design, trace it onto paper or photocopy it if possible. Enlarge or reduce the design until it is the size needed to fit the area where you plan to use it. Next, transfer designs from the paper to fabric. You will need a light source with a writing surface, such as a light box. If you do not have a light box, there are several other options, such as the following suggestions:

- Open up your dining room table and place a piece of glass over the opening. Place a lamp under the glass, making sure to remove the lamp shade.

- Tape the design to a window and use the sun as your light source.
- Tape the design to the TV screen. Turn off the sound and turn to a "snowy" channel—one without a program.

Remember to use an appropriate marker when transferring designs and test the marker for removability before use. See "Marking Tools" on page 21.

 One of my students gave me this great suggestion for tracing designs from a book without damaging the book. Place a piece of wax paper over the design; then place a piece of tracing paper over the wax paper. Using a fine-line marker, trace the design.

Some quilting designs do not need a drawn or traced design. This completely random method of stitching is called meander quilting.

Stippling is a popular meander quilting design that resembles a series of closely spaced hills and bumps that meander across the area, never crossing each other. The size of the hills and bumps is determined by the size of the space to be quilted. Stippling is particularly suited to trapunto work because the stitches can be placed close together to accentuate the raised design.

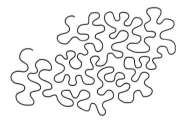

Stippling is a learned skill that requires practice. For a beginner, it helps to draw the design on paper first. Once you've achieved satisfactory shapes on paper, insert an old needle into your machine and practice stitching on a blank sheet of paper before advancing to fabric.

For practice, try this exercise: take a square of paper and mark a grid with 1" squares on it. Within one grid square draw a series of two or three bumps that go in the same direction; then turn in another direction and make two or three more bumps. Fill one grid square before advancing to the next one. Continue shifting directions. Be careful not to box yourself into a corner or cross over any lines.

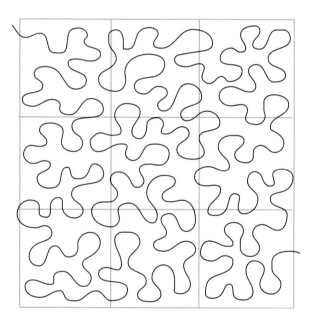

Keep the units or bumps clustered and branch out slowly. Long rows of bumps that do not shift direction can cause fabric distortion.

Don't do this:

or

To keep track of where you are going and to prevent crossover, keep an empty field behind the needle and always stitch in that direction.

We are trained from childhood to read and write from left to right, making it awkward to go from right to left. If you find you are having trouble making smooth curves when going from right to left, try the following exercise. Once you can master this exercise on paper, working on fabric will be no problem.

1. With a pencil and paper, draw continuous circles from left to right. Draw the next row from right to left.

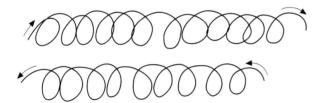

2. Draw L-shaped loops from left to right; then from right to left.

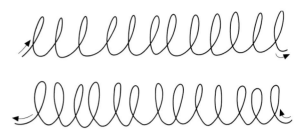

3. Insert an old needle into your sewing machine and practice stitching the shapes on a blank sheet of paper.
4. Thread the machine and practice on a fabric "sandwich" that consists of one layer each of fashion fabric, batting, and backing.

Orchid Sky

Combine free-motion and machine-guided quilting in this simple yet elegant vest. Made from silk douppioni, it is lined to the edge, where a twisted thread trim provides a finishing touch. The orchid design is adapted from Japanese Design Motifs, *translated by Fumie Adachi (Dover Publications, 1972).*

MATERIALS

- Vest pattern of your choice with plain or darted front and back, and center front edge closure
- Medium-weight silk or quilting cotton for the vest fashion fabric. To determine the yardage needed, do a mock layout with the front and back pieces. Leave enough space between the pieces to cut them out 1" larger than the patterns. Because this vest is lined to the edge, ignore any facing pieces that may be called for in the pattern.
- Lightweight cotton or cotton/polyester blend for the backing in a neutral color. Determine the yardage in the same manner as for the fashion fabric.
- Coordinating lining fabric in the yardage indicated on the pattern envelope for the vest fashion fabric. Because the garment is lined to the edge, the lining yardage is calculated by using the fashion fabric requirements.
- Batting. Begin with a thinner batting listed on page 27. If the desired look is not achieved, test other battings until you find a batting that gives the desired results. To determine the yardage required, do a mock layout with the front and back pieces. Leave enough space between the pieces to cut them 1" larger than the patterns.
- Threads: all-purpose for construction in a color that matches fashion fabric, 40-weight rayon for channel quilting in a color that matches fashion fabric, metallic for quilting the orchid motif in a

To keep track of where you are going and to prevent crossover, keep an empty field behind the needle and always stitch in that direction.

We are trained from childhood to read and write from left to right, making it awkward to go from right to left. If you find you are having trouble making smooth curves when going from right to left, try the following exercise. Once you can master this exercise on paper, working on fabric will be no problem.

1. With a pencil and paper, draw continuous circles from left to right. Draw the next row from right to left.

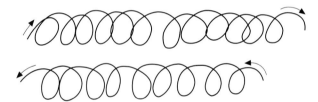

2. Draw L-shaped loops from left to right; then from right to left.

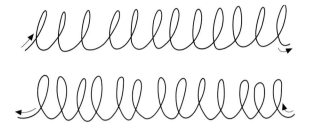

3. Insert an old needle into your sewing machine and practice stitching the shapes on a blank sheet of paper.

4. Thread the machine and practice on a fabric "sandwich" that consists of one layer each of fashion fabric, batting, and backing.

Orchid Sky

Combine free-motion and machine-guided quilting in this simple yet elegant vest. Made from silk douppioni, it is lined to the edge, where a twisted thread trim provides a finishing touch. The orchid design is adapted from Japanese Design Motifs, *translated by Fumie Adachi (Dover Publications, 1972).*

MATERIALS

- Vest pattern of your choice with plain or darted front and back, and center front edge closure
- Medium-weight silk or quilting cotton for the vest fashion fabric. To determine the yardage needed, do a mock layout with the front and back pieces. Leave enough space between the pieces to cut them out 1" larger than the patterns. Because this vest is lined to the edge, ignore any facing pieces that may be called for in the pattern.
- Lightweight cotton or cotton/polyester blend for the backing in a neutral color. Determine the yardage in the same manner as for the fashion fabric.
- Coordinating lining fabric in the yardage indicated on the pattern envelope for the vest fashion fabric. Because the garment is lined to the edge, the lining yardage is calculated by using the fashion fabric requirements.
- Batting. Begin with a thinner batting listed on page 27. If the desired look is not achieved, test other battings until you find a batting that gives the desired results. To determine the yardage required, do a mock layout with the front and back pieces. Leave enough space between the pieces to cut them 1" larger than the patterns.
- Threads: all-purpose for construction in a color that matches fashion fabric, 40-weight rayon for channel quilting in a color that matches fashion fabric, metallic for quilting the orchid motif in a

color that matches fashion fabric, invisible monofilament for braid application, 2 skeins of #5 pearl cotton for braid in a color to match fashion fabric

- Needles: 80/12 universal for construction, 80/12 metallic for metallic thread, 75/11 embroidery for rayon thread
- Other materials: darning foot; walking foot; marking tool; glass-head straight pins; thread-twisting tool, such as The Spinster described on page 104, for making edge braid; buttons as called for on the pattern envelope; tracing paper

INSTRUCTIONS

1. Prewash or dry-clean the fashion fabric, backing, and lining fabrics according to the manufacturer's instructions, if desired. Press out any wrinkles.

2. From the fashion fabric, batting, and backing fabric, cut the vest front and back pieces. Cut them 1" larger than the patterns. Because this vest is lined to the edges, ignore any facing pieces that may be called for in the pattern and use the vest front and back patterns to cut the lining pieces.

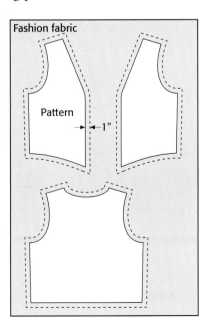

Tip — Mark the seam allowance lines on the fashion fabric pieces before removing the pattern so you can use them as a reference point when placing design motifs.

3. Using the marking tool, transfer the grain line to the fashion fabric pieces.

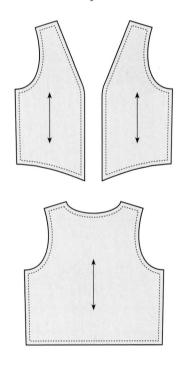

4. Transfer the orchid motifs on page 35 to tracing paper and then to the right side of the fashion fabric pieces as shown, placing the smaller orchid at the neck edge and the larger orchid at the hip. Using the grain line as a reference point, draw vertical lines 1" apart on the front and back pieces. Do not draw through the orchid motifs.

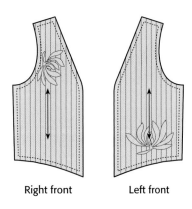

Right front   Left front

Back

5. Layer the front and back pieces in the following order: backing, right side down; batting; fashion fabric, right side up.

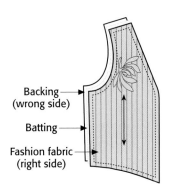

Backing (wrong side)

Batting

Fashion fabric (right side)

6. Pin-baste every 2" to 4", depending on the batting used. If possible, avoid pinning where there are stitching lines.

7. Refer to "Machine Setup and Stitching Techniques" on page 14 to set up the machine for free-motion quilting. Insert the metallic needle. Thread the needle with the metallic thread and wind the bobbin with all-purpose thread. After you make test samples and determine that the stitch length and tension are satisfactory, stitch the orchid motif lines of each piece.

8. Refer to "Machine Setup and Stitching Techniques" on page 14 to set up the machine for machine-guided stitching. Remove the metallic needle and insert the embroidery needle. Attach the walking foot. Thread the needle with rayon thread. After you make test samples and determine that the tension is satisfactory, stitch the straight lines on each piece, beginning with the center line. As you approach an orchid motif, follow the stitched lines of the motif until you are $\frac{1}{8}$" away from the straight-stitched line. With the needle in the fabric, turn the garment so you will be stitching in the opposite direction. Place the inside edge of the walking foot close to the straight-stitched line. Stitch back to the edge of the piece. Repeat until all of the double lines have been stitched.

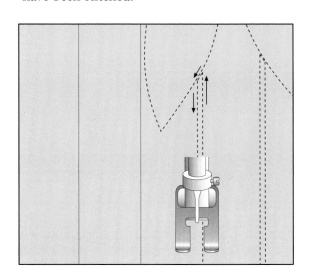

9. If the fabrics were not prewashed in step 1, finish the raw edges of each piece with serging or a zigzag stitch. Wash and dry the pieces.

10. Lay the appropriate pattern on each quilted piece. Cut out each piece along the pattern edges.

11. Follow the pattern instructions to stitch the front to the back at the shoulder seams. Refer to "Easy Vest Lining" on page 109 to assemble the lining and line the vest, leaving a 1" to 1½" opening at the center back neckline and lower edges. Using the pearl cotton, refer to "Making Spinster Braid" on page 104 to make Spinster braids. Follow the instructions in "Mock Piping" on page 103 to stitch the braid to the vest outer edges with invisible thread, forming Sew-As-You-Go loop closures on the vest right front as instructed in "Button Loop Closures" on page 106.

12. Position the buttons on the vest left front to correspond with the loop closure placements, and sew the buttons to the vest.

Orchid Sky
Patterns

Bobbin or Reverse Quilting

I n this method of quilting, the quilt "sandwich" (fashion fabric, batting, backing, and/or lining) is reversed: the right side of the fashion fabric is against the throat plate and the backing is closest to the needle. This type of quilting is good for transferring the design of a print fabric to a solid fabric, such as in the examples "Swallows in Flight" (below) and the vest from "Evening Tango" (page 49). Select a bobbin thread appropriate for the design and fabric.

Swallows in Flight

How do you mix one print fabric with one solid fabric and end up with one simply smashing reversible vest? Bobbin quilting is the answer, and it is so easy to do.

MATERIALS

- Any style of vest pattern with front button closure
- Medium-weight, solid-color, 100 percent cotton for the fashion fabric; coordinating cotton print with easily distinguished motifs for the lining. Because this vest is reversible, we will refer to the solid-color fabric as the fashion fabric and the print fabric as the lining to avoid confusion. To determine the yardage required, do a mock layout with the front and back pattern pieces, leaving enough space between the pieces to cut them out 1" larger than the pattern. Because this vest is lined to the edges and bound, ignore any facing pieces that may be called for in the pattern. Purchase ½ yard extra of the solid-color fabric for the binding.
- Batting. Begin with a thinner batting listed on page 27. If the desired look is not achieved, test other battings until you find a batting that gives the desired results. To determine the yardage required, do a mock layout with the front and back pieces. Leave enough space between the pieces to cut them 1" larger than the patterns.
- Threads: all-purpose for construction in a color that matches fashion fabric, 30- or 40-weight rayon in a color to match or contrast with fashion fabric, invisible monofilament
- Needles: 80/12 universal for construction, 75/11 quilting for invisible monofilament thread
- Other materials: darning foot, glass-head straight pins, buttons as called for on the pattern envelope

INSTRUCTIONS

1. Prewash the fashion and lining fabrics according to the manufacturer's instructions, if desired. Press out any wrinkles.
2. From the fashion fabric, batting, and lining, cut the vest front and back pieces, cutting them 1" larger than the patterns. Because this vest is reversible, ignore any facing pieces that may be called for in the pattern.

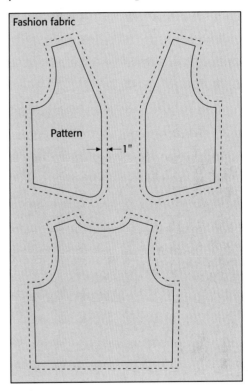

3. Layer the front and back pieces in the following order: fashion fabric, right side down; batting; lining, right side up.

4. Pin-baste every 2" to 4", depending on the batting used.

5. Referring to "Machine Setup and Stitching Techniques" on page 14, set up the machine for free-motion stitching. Insert the quilting needle into the machine. Thread the needle with invisible monofilament thread and wind the bobbin with rayon thread that matches or contrasts with the fashion fabric.

 To avoid tangled threads under your fabric, lower the presser foot, take one stitch, and pull up the bobbin thread each time you begin a new line of stitching. Hold the top and bobbin thread to the left of the presser foot; continue stitching. Please note that this is not necessary when dragging the threads from one motif to another.

6. After you have made test samples and determined that the tension is satisfactory, quilt the layers of each piece together, stitching around the motifs of the lining fabric. If the fabric design is made up of individual motifs, like the swallows on the sample vest shown here, lock the threads at the beginning and end of each motif. I find that it works well to stitch ¼" of small stitches at the beginning and end of each design. Without cutting the threads, I

 Start and stop your locking stitches at a point rather than a straight edge and they will be less noticeable.

then raise the presser foot and drag the threads to the next motif and repeat the stitching process. Clip the threads when all of the motifs have been stitched.

7. If the fabrics were not prewashed in step 1, finish the raw edges of each piece with serging or a zigzag stitch. Wash and dry the pieces.

8. Lay the appropriate pattern on each quilted piece. Cut out each piece along the pattern edges.

9. Refer to "Seam Finishes" on page 108 to stitch the garment together. Use either a flat-felled or bias-bound seam finish.

10. Follow the pattern instructions to stitch the garment together and to make the buttonholes in the vest right front.

11. Refer to "Edge Finishes" on page 100 to make bias binding from the fashion fabric and bind the outer raw edges.

12. Position the buttons on the vest left front to correspond with the buttonhole placement, and sew the buttons to the vest.

 Before beginning to stitch, use the sewing-machine hand wheel to set the needle into the fabric.

Trapunto

Trapunto, once called stuffed work, is an age-old technique where an appliqué or quilted motif is stuffed with extra batting to give it a high-relief texture. This technique used to require slitting the back of a motif and inserting extra batting; however, with the invention of water-soluble thread, trapunto has been simplified to a noninvasive technique. Rather than slitting the backing to insert the batting, a layer of thick batting is placed under the trapunto design and basted in place with water-soluble thread. After the excess thicker batting is trimmed away, a thinner batting is placed under the whole piece. The design is then stitched around with all-purpose thread and the open areas are quilted with a stitch that fills the area. To accent the trapunto design even more, the open areas are quilted by using a dense quilting stitch like stippling (see page 30). Other dense or fill stitches, like rail fence, snail's trail or cabbage rose, and feather, are also good.

Solid-color fabrics show trapunto better than print fabrics.

Even channel stitching (see page 29), using the edge of the darning foot as a guide, can densely fill the areas around a trapunto design. For larger areas, consider a meandering loop design. Once you have finished quilting, rinse or spritz your fabric piece with water to remove the water-soluble thread.

Meandering Loop

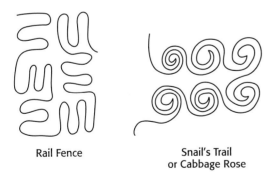

Rail Fence

Snail's Trail
or Cabbage Rose

Feather

Store unused, water-soluble thread in a resealable plastic bag so that the moisture in the air will not damage it.

Sunshine

Kiss dreary days good-bye when you wear this linen dress with its happy sunshine face. It's guaranteed to give you a bright outlook. The dimensional bodice design is achieved with a layer of cotton/polyester batting and secured with self-lining.

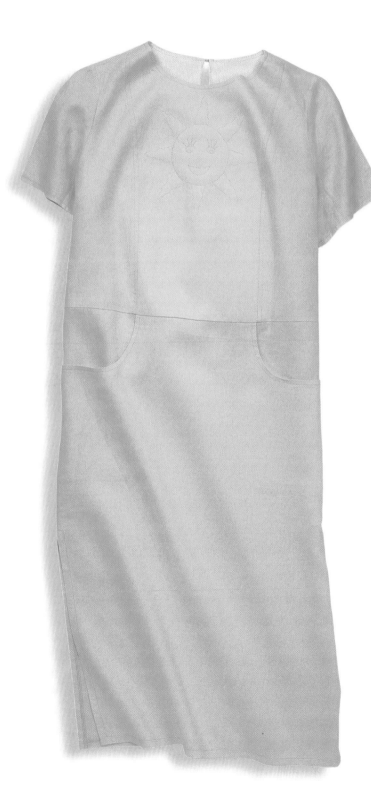

MATERIALS

- Jumper or dress pattern with plain, attached bodice
- Solid-color cotton or machine-washable linen in the yardage indicated on the pattern envelope, plus extra for lining the bodice front
- 12" x 12" piece of low-loft polyester or cotton/polyester batting (refer to the chart on page 27)
- Threads: all-purpose for construction in a color to match fashion fabric, water-soluble basting, 30- or 40-weight rayon in a color to match fashion fabric
- Needles: 75/11 universal for construction, 75/11 embroidery for rayon thread
- Other materials: tracing paper, glass-head straight pins, darning foot, water-soluble marker, 4" embroidery scissors, other notions as called for on the pattern envelope

INSTRUCTIONS

1. Prewash or dry-clean the fabric according to the manufacturer's instructions. Cut out all of the pieces according to the pattern instructions. Cut an additional front bodice piece to use as the lining.

2. Transfer the sun design on page 43 to tracing paper. Using a water-soluble marker, transfer the design to the center of the bodice.

3. Place the batting on the wrong side of the bodice, under the design. Pin-baste the batting in place, pinning every ½" to 1".

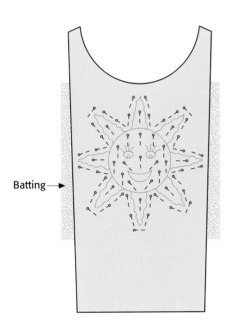

Batting →

4. Refer to "Machine Setup and Stitching Techniques" on page 14 to set up the machine for free-motion quilting. Insert the universal needle. Thread the needle and wind the bobbin with water-soluble thread.

5. Baste on the outer lines of the design. The stitching is only temporary, so there is no reason to worry about even stitches.

6. Working on the wrong side of the garment, use 4" scissors to trim away the excess batting beyond the stitching line. Trim as close as possible to the stitching line. Be careful not to cut into the fashion fabric.

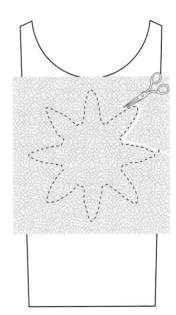

7. With wrong sides together, place the bodice lining and bodice together. Pin the pieces together with straight pins, starting in the center of the motif. Place the pins every ½" to 1" inside and around the design motif, and every 2" to 3" outside the design.

8. Remove the universal needle from the machine and replace it with the embroidery needle. Thread the needle with rayon thread and wind the bobbin with all-purpose thread.

9. With the machine still set up for free-motion stitching, stitch on all of the design lines, including the lines that were previously basted. Stitch out from the center of the design. Remove the pins as you sew to avoid stitching over them.

10. When the stitching is completed, soak the bodice front in water to remove the basting thread and marker lines.

11. Follow the pattern instructions to complete the dress.

Sunshine
Pattern

Persian Plaid

Solid cotton fabrics provide the ideal canvas for this reversible vest made with the trapunto technique, while a striking plaid for the pants and vest binding complements the vest. The floral design for trapunto is adapted from Traditional Floral Designs and Motifs for Artists and Craftspeople *by Madeleine Orban-Szontagh (Dover Publications, 1989). Quilted with unwashed fabrics and cotton batting, this vest is a good example of the old-fashioned puckered texture that results after washing.*

MATERIALS

- Plain-front vest and pants patterns of your choice
- Plaid fabric for slacks in yardage indicated on the pattern envelope, plus ½ yard additional for vest bias binding
- Two solid-color cottons, one for the vest fashion fabric and one for the lining, in colors that coordinate with the plaid. Because this vest is reversible, we will refer to the light solid color as the fashion fabric and the dark as the lining to avoid confusion. To determine the yardage required, do a mock layout with the vest pieces, leaving enough space between the pieces to cut them 1" larger than the patterns. Because this vest is lined to the edges and bound, ignore any facing pieces that may be called for in the pattern.
- Battings: ½ yard of thick batting for the trapunto designs; thin batting for the vest fronts and back. To determine the yardage required for the thin batting, do a mock layout with the front and back pieces. Leave enough space between the pieces to cut them out 1" larger than the patterns. See page 27 for batting suggestions.
- Threads: all-purpose for construction in colors to match fashion fabrics, water-soluble for trapunto basting, rayon for trapunto stitching in colors to match each vest fabric, invisible monofilament for quilting
- Needles: 75/11 universal for construction, 75/11 embroidery for rayon thread, 75/11 quilting for invisible monofilament thread
- Other materials: darning foot, glass-head straight pins, water-soluble fabric marker, tracing paper, 4" embroidery scissors, other notions as called for on the pattern envelopes

INSTRUCTIONS

1. Prewash or dry-clean the plaid fabric according to the manufacturer's instructions; leave the solid-color vest fabrics unwashed. Press out any wrinkles.
2. Cut out and construct the pants according to the pattern instructions.
3. From the fashion fabric, thin batting, and lining, cut the vest front and back pieces 1" larger than the patterns. Because this vest is reversible, ignore any facing pieces that may be called for in the pattern. With a water-soluble marker, mark the seam allowance lines on the vest fashion fabric (light fabric).

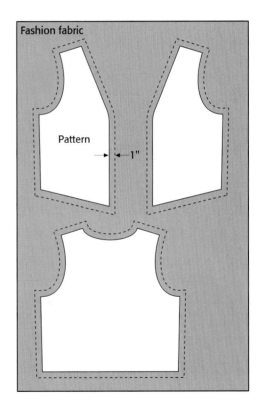

4. Trace the design on page 47 onto tracing paper. With a water-soluble marker, transfer the design to the tracing paper and then to the right sides of the vest fashion fabric fronts (light) and back as shown.

5. Place the thick batting on the wrong sides of the vest pieces under the design. Pin-baste the batting in place, pinning every ½" to 1" and around design.

6. Refer to "Machine Setup and Stitching Techniques" on page 14 to set up the machine for free-motion quilting. Insert the universal needle. Thread the needle and wind the bobbin with water-soluble thread.

7. Stitch on the outer lines of the design. The stitching is only temporary, so there is no reason to worry about even stitches.

8. Working on the wrong side of each piece, use the 4" scissors to trim away the excess batting beyond the stitching line. Trim as close as possible to the stitching line. Be careful not to cut into the fashion fabric. See page 41 for an example.

9. Layer the front and back pieces in the following order: lining, right side down; thin batting; fashion fabric, right side up. Pin the pieces together with straight pins, starting in the center of the motifs. Place the pins every ½" to 1" inside and around the design motifs, and every 2" to 3" outside the designs.

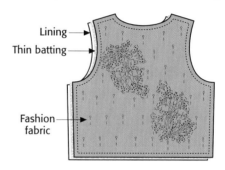

Lining

Thin batting

Fashion fabric

10. Remove the universal needle from the machine and replace it with the embroidery needle. Thread the needle with dark rayon thread in a color that matches the lining fabric; wind the bobbin with light rayon thread that matches the fashion fabric.

11. With the machine still set up for free-motion stitching, stitch on all of the design lines, including the lines that were previously basted. Remove the pins as you sew to avoid stitching over them.

12. Replace the embroidery needle with the quilting needle. Thread the needle and wind the bobbin with invisible monofilament thread. Use smoke color in the bobbin and clear on top for stippling the background areas. Refer to "Quilting Designs" on page 28 to stipple quilt.

13. Finish the raw edges of each piece with serging or a zigzag stitch. Soak the quilted pieces in water to remove the basting thread and marker lines, then machine wash and dry each piece.

14. Lay the appropriate pattern on each quilted piece. Cut out each piece along the pattern edges.

15. Refer to "Seam Finishes" on page 108 and the pattern instructions to stitch the garment together. Use a flat-felled seam finish.

16. Refer to "Making Continuous Bias Binding" on page 102 and "Edge Finishes" on page 100 to make binding from the plaid fabric and bind the outer raw edges of the vest.

Persian Plaid
Pattern

Machine Quilting
PHOTO GALLERY

Senior Prom

Stipple quilting with rayon thread in the needle and bobbin turned this inexpensive polyester fabric into a sophisticated party dress. The pieces were cut out and then layered with Mountain Mist Low Loft polyester batting, which was reduced to half its thickness by splitting it in half before quilting.

Winterblooms

The quilting design on the collar, hem, and sleeves is from *1001 Floral Motifs and Ornaments for Artists and Craftspeople,* a Dover publication edited by Carol Belanger Grafton. After enlarging and manipulating the design to fit the desired spaces, it was transferred to muslin backing pieces. The backing, batting, and wool pieces were layered and bobbin quilted with sliver metallic thread. Straight lines were quilted on

this garment with the machine-guided technique. The floral and crosshatch designs were then free-motion quilted. The vest appliqués were cut from silk, Ultra Suede, and wool; then fused to the vest with paper-backed fusible web. The flowers, vines, and leaves were stitched in place with a blanket stitch and contrasting rayon threads. The triangle border edges were couched with a metallic braid and thread. This ensemble received first place in both the 1996 AQS Fashion Show and Contest, and the 1996 Pennsylvania National Quilt Extravaganza Wearables Show.

Evening Tango

The velvet portions of the jacket were broomsticked (see page 52); then threadwork was added (see page 72). The paisley design on the reverse side of the metallic fabric on the jacket body was quilted with the trapunto technique. I made a coordinating vest, and the outfit received first place at both the 1996 Mid-Atlantic Wearable Art Festival II and the Dallas Quilt Celebration. It also received second place at the 1996 East Coast Quilter's Alliance Made-to-Wear Show.

Baby, It's Cold Outside

Machine trapunto snowflakes float across the body of this satin coat. The pattern is from *Ready to Use Snowflake Designs* by Mack Fraga, published by Dover Publications. The velvet used in the lapels and cuffs was broomsticked, stabilized, and embellished with threads and cords from Sulky and Kreinik. The skirt, camisole, and hat were also created by using the same techniques. This ensemble was shown at the 1996/1997 Fairfield Fashion Show.

Town and Country

The jacket center fronts and backs were free-motion quilted with a fleur-de-lis design between the lattice appliqué work. The fleur-de-lis theme on the garment was taken from the jacket lining. The side fronts, backs, sleeves, and hat were machine channel quilted by using alternating rows of straight and feather stitch. The backing fabric was a very loose weave, cotton-blend fabric. All red braid trim was couched. Not shown is a coordinating vest. "Town and Country" received first place at three different shows: the 1997 AQS Fashion Show and Contest, the 1997 IQA Show, and the 1998 Mid-Atlantic Wearable Art Show.

Fabric Manipulation

Twist it, scrunch it, squash it, stitch it—there are all kinds of ways to manipulate fabric to achieve texture. In this chapter we explore the creative techniques of broomsticking, origami puffs, seamless patchwork, pintucking, and twisted tucks—but don't stop with these. Try mixing them with techniques found in other chapters for your own unique fabric creations.

Broomsticking

I first saw this texturing technique on a garment created by Linda McGehee. If you're familiar with her work, you're already well acquainted with broomsticking. It is great all by itself or combined with other techniques to add visual interest. The blouse project presented in this chapter features a solid-color fabric broomsticked and embellished with decorative threads. For other examples, refer to the photo gallery on page 69 as well as garments in other chapters where broomsticking is combined with other techniques.

The broomsticking process involves wetting a natural-fiber fabric, twisting it, drying it, and then stabilizing it with fusible interfacing to make a new, unique piece of fabric. Cotton, silk, wool, linen, and rayon or acetate (both are synthetics made from cellulose) work well with this technique. Don't worry if your fabric label says it can only be dry-cleaned. I have successfully done this technique with every kind of fabric, from quilting cotton to expensive rayon velvet.

Be aware that with this technique you need more fabric than called for on the pattern envelope because the width of the fabric decreases. Standard 44"/45"-wide quilting fabric shrinks to approximately 30"; rayon acetate, also known as baroque satin, also shrinks from 45" to 30". Lighter fabrics usually shrink more, while heavier fabrics usually shrink less. You do, however, have control over how much shrinkage there is by how much or how little you stretch the wrinkled fabric. Do a mock layout with your pattern pieces to calculate how much fabric to purchase by using 30" as a guideline. Depending on the pattern size used, you usually can get the front out of one width of fabric and the back out of a second width of fabric, but the sleeves require two widths. I purchase $\frac{1}{4}$ yard extra beyond my calculations just to be sure I have enough. For example, if I were making a blouse and the blouse front was 24" long, the back was 26" long, and each sleeve was 25" long, I would need 3 yards of fabric (24" + 26" + 25" + 25" + 9" = 109" divided by 36" = 3 yards of fabric).

In addition to the fabric you choose, the type of interfacing you select also affects the finished product. A woven-cotton, fusible interfacing will give a finished product body. Tricot fusible interfacing creates a fabric that drapes. In order to make the right decision, it is always better to do a few tests with your broomsticked fabric and several different interfacings.

Holiday Cheer

Who would have thought that a plain rayon acetate fabric could be wadded up and look this elegant? Broomsticking turns even a simple pattern like this slit-front blouse into a garment fit for a holiday fete.

MATERIALS

- Blouse pattern of your choice
- 45"-wide rayon/acetate satin. To determine the yardage required, do a mock layout with the pattern pieces. Use a 30" width for your calculations.
- Fusible tricot interfacing. To determine the yardage required, divide the fabric yardage (in inches) by the interfacing width. Multiply that number by the width of the finished broomsticked fabric. Round up the number to the nearest whole number. Multiply by the broomsticked fabric width and divide the number by 36. For example, if you needed 3 yards (108") of fabric and the interfacing was 22" wide, you would need to purchase 4¼ yards of interfacing (108" ÷ 22" = 4.9 lengths [round to 5]; 5 lengths x 30" = 150" ÷ 36 = 4.16 yards [round up to 4¼]).
- Threads: all-purpose for construction, decorative threads/cords of your choice for embellishing, invisible monofilament and/or rayon for applying the decorative threads
- Needles: 80/12 universal for construction, 80/12 metallic for metallic threads
- Other materials: 4 to 6 rubber bands, glass-head straight pins, other notions as called for on the pattern envelope

INSTRUCTIONS

1. Prewash the interfacing according to the manufacturer's instructions. Place the fashion fabric in the washer and run it through the rinse and spin cycles only.

2. Take a cut end of the wet fashion fabric and accordion pleat it into 1" pleats across the fabric width. Secure each end with a rubber band.

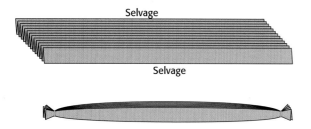

3. Place a rubber-banded end under your foot to hold it in place and start twisting the other end with your hands until it twists itself into a rope and then into a ball. (This method can be done with about two yards of fabric, depending on how tall you are. For longer lengths, have a friend hold an end while you twist.) Use rubber bands to hold the ball in place.

4. Place the twisted ball on or near a heat source and let it dry. I use the warmest radiator in the house and the ball dries in a couple of days, even with a dish towel under the fabric to protect it. Another place to let it dry is in front of or on top of a forced-air register. Use caution when drying the twisted ball, however, so that you do not scorch the fabric or cause it to catch fire. In the summer, I place it in a lingerie bag and hang it outside. The dryer is always an option, too. Do not use a microwave or conventional oven.

5. When the fabric is dry, remove the rubber bands and carefully open the ball of dried fabric. It will naturally unfold to about 30". With the wrong side up, place the fabric on an ironing board so that a selvage edge is aligned with the far edge of the board. Insert approximately 4 pins through the fabric and into the board to hold it in place.

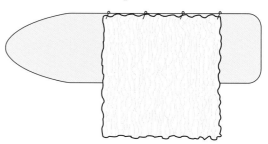

6. Cut the prewashed interfacing into lengths the width of the broomsticked fabric (approximately 30"). Place a length of interfacing across the width of the fabric with the resin side against the wrong side of the fabric. Follow the manufacturer's instructions to fuse the interfacing to the fabric. Butt or overlap the next piece of interfacing ¼" and fuse. Repeat for the entire piece. Press the finished piece from the right side.

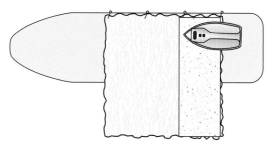

7. Cut the blouse pieces from the broomsticked fabric.

8. Refer to "Machine Setup and Stitching Techniques" on page 14 to set up the machine for regular sewing. Using invisible or rayon thread and a needle appropriate for the thread, refer to "Threadwork and Couching" on page 72 to stitch the decorative threads to the right side of the blouse pieces in random, gently curving lines.

Note: I USED THREE DIFFERENT TYPES OF KREINIK THREAD AND DECORATIVE CORDS FOR THIS PROJECT. BLENDING FILAMENT WAS STITCHED DIRECTLY TO THE FABRIC WITH A STRAIGHT STITCH. JAPAN THREAD WAS SEWN DIRECTLY TO THE FABRIC WITH A DECORATIVE FEATHER STITCH. OMBRE THREAD OR CORD WAS TOO THICK TO GO THROUGH A NEEDLE SO IT WAS COUCHED TO THE FABRIC WITH INVISIBLE THREAD.

Tip If the garment pieces appear slightly distorted, steam-press them and they will lie flat.

9. Follow the pattern instructions to complete the garment.

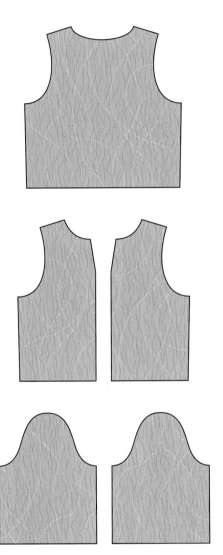

Holiday Cheer detail

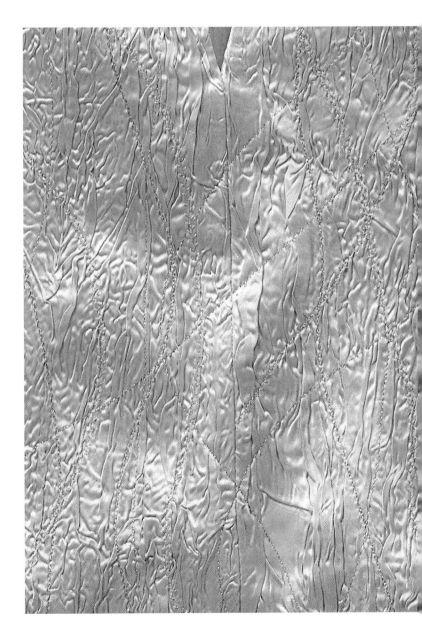

Origami Puffs

In this technique developed by Doris Van Kalker of Germany, fabric squares are textured and then added to a garment. The basic technique involves using a square of fabric and a square of paper-backed fusible web cut smaller than the fabric. The corners of the fabric are fused to the corners of the fusible web to create a puff, and then the entire piece is "smashed" with an iron. What a great way to work out your frustrations!

MATERIALS

- Any style of vest pattern with front button closure
- Solid-color, medium-weight cotton, taffeta, silk, linen, or denim for the vest fashion fabric. To determine the yardage needed, do a mock layout with the front and back pieces. Because this vest is lined to the edge and bound, ignore any facing pieces that may be called for in the pattern.

Origami Patch Vest

You'll be a smashing success wherever you wear this embellished vest. The original was part of a three-piece ensemble named "Afternoon Delight" that was entered in the 1997/98 Hoffman Challenge and won second place. The vest features origami puffs on a thread-embellished background.

- Coordinating lining fabric. Determine the yardage in the same manner as for the fashion fabric.
- ¼ yard *each* of 3 to 5 fabrics that coordinate with the vest fashion fabric for the origami patches. Purchase an extra ½ yard of one of the fabrics for the bias binding.
- Fusible woven interfacing. To determine the yardage needed, do a mock layout with the vest pattern pieces, ignoring any facing pieces that may be called for in the pattern. If you are working with a 22"-wide interfacing, refer to "Interfacings" on page 11.
- Threads: all-purpose for construction, 2 or 3 colors of rayon in colors to coordinate with puff fabrics, invisible monofilament
- Needles: 80/12 universal for invisible thread construction of garment and, 80/12 topstitching for double rayon thread, 75/11 embroidery for single rayon thread
- Other materials: ½ yard of paper-backed fusible web, darning foot, coordinating rattail cord for vest edges, buttons as called for on the pattern envelope

INSTRUCTIONS

1. Prewash or dry-clean the fabrics and interfacing according to the manufacturer's instructions.
2. From the vest fabric, lining, and interfacing, cut the front and back pieces. Because this vest is lined to the edge and bound, ignore any facing pieces that may be called for in the pattern. If you are working with a 22"-wide interfacing, refer to "Interfacings" on page 11 to join 2 pieces so that they are large enough to fit the vest back pattern.

3. Fuse the interfacing pieces to the wrong side of the fashion fabric pieces.
4. Refer to "Machine Setup and Stitching Techniques" on page 14 to set up the machine for regular sewing. Insert the embroidery needle into the machine. Using one of the rayon thread colors in the needle and all-purpose thread in the bobbin, stitch several rows of gently curving lines the length of the garment pieces. Repeat the process with the remaining rayon thread colors.

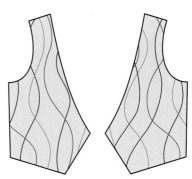

 A walking foot helps prevent fabric distortion when sewing the decorative rows.

5. Insert the universal needle into the machine. With all-purpose thread in the needle and bobbin, follow the pattern instructions to stitch the front and back pieces together at the side seams. Press the seam allowances open.

6. To make the origami puffs, cut 10 to 12 squares (amount will depend on preference and vest size), each 4" x 4", from the puff fabrics. Cut an equal number of squares, each 3" x 3", from the fusible web. Place the fusible web squares on an ironing surface, resin sides up. With a dry iron set at the recommended temperature, iron the wrong side of each corner of a fabric square to the corresponding corner of a fusible web square. The result will be a puffy looking object. Gently smash the puff with the heated iron, or, if desired, arrange the excess fabric first, and then smash it with the iron. Repeat for the remaining fabric and fusible web squares. Allow the square to cool.

4" x 4" fabric

3" x 3" fusible web

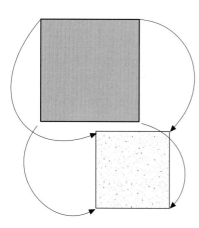

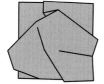

7. Remove the paper backing from each square. Position the puffs as desired around the bottom of the entire vest, on the right side of the vest pieces. Follow the manufacturer's instructions to fuse the squares in place.

8. Refer to "Machine Setup and Stitching Techniques" on page 14 to set up the machine for free-motion stitching. Insert the topstitching needle into your machine. Referring to "Sewing with Twin and Triple Needles" on page 00, thread the needle with two of the rayon threads and wind the bobbin with all-purpose thread.

9. Using an irregular, side-to-side zigzag motion, straight stitch back and forth along the edges of each square.

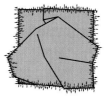

10. Return the machine setup to regular sewing. Stitch the vest front and back together at the shoulder seams. Stitch the lining front and back together at the side and shoulder seams, right sides together. Press open. Slide the lining into the vest, wrong sides together. Stitch all raw edges together with a ⅝" seam allowance.

11. Refer to "Making Continuous Bias Binding" on page 102 and "Bias Binding" on page 101 to make bias binding from the binding fabric and apply it to the vest outer edges. Leave an opening in the binding seam at the center back neckline to insert the rattail cord.

12. Follow the instructions in "Threadwork and Couching" on page 72 to stitch the rattail cord along the seam edges between the vest and binding fabric with invisible thread. Follow the instructions in "Mock Piping" on page 103 to insert the cord ends into the center back opening.

13. Follow the pattern instructions to make the buttonholes and attach the buttons.

Seamless Patchwork

S eamless patchwork is another technique developed by Doris Van Kalker. It looks like patchwork but is much easier because the pieces are fused together rather than stitched. Many types of fabrics will work for this technique, even lightweight home decorating fabrics. I have made complete garments with this technique, but my favorite thing is to combine it with fabric manipulation for a really elegant look.

To make seamless patchwork, fabric squares and rectangles are laid on a fusible base with their raw edges butted together. The pieces are then fused and the raw edges are covered with stitching. The pieces can then be further embellished if desired.

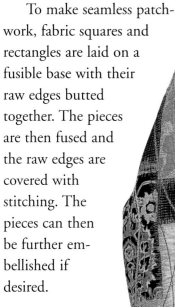

Black and Tan

These neutral fabrics won't stand in a corner and go unnoticed. With decorative stitching embellishing the seamless patchwork, all eyes will be on you when you walk into a room wearing this striking jacket.

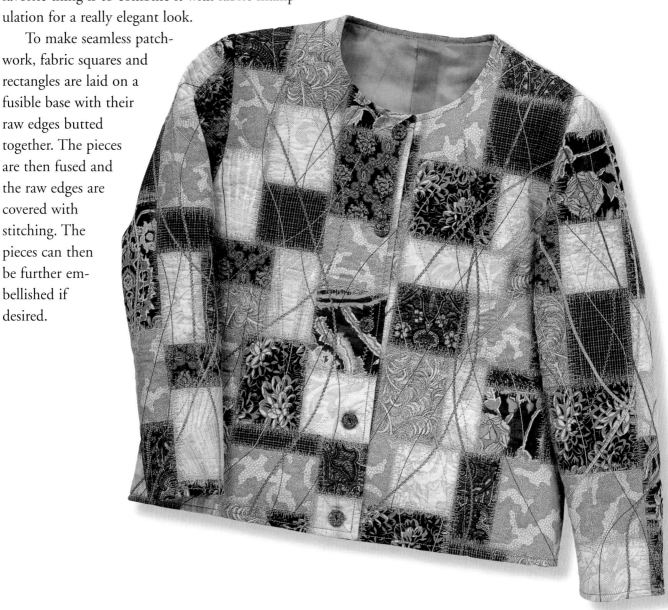

MATERIALS

- Any style of lined jacket pattern
- A minimum of 8 different fabrics for the patchwork. To determine the yardage required for each fabric, divide the amount of yardage called for on the pattern envelope by the number of fabrics. Round up to the nearest ⅛ yard. For example: If the jacket requires 2½ yards and you have 8 fabrics, you will need ⅜ yard of each fabric (2.5 ÷ 8 = .312).
- Coordinating lining fabric in the yardage indicated on the pattern envelope
- Fusible woven interfacing. To determine the yardage needed, do a mock layout with the jacket pattern pieces. Ignore any facing pieces that may be called for in the pattern. If you are working with a 22"-wide interfacing, refer to "Interfacings" on page 11.
- Threads: all-purpose for construction in a color to match fabrics, plus 2 colors that coordinate with the patchwork fabrics for sealing the patches; variety of decorative threads, ribbons, and yarns for embellishing; bobbin
- Needles: 80/12 universal for construction, 75/11 embroidery for decorative threads, 80/12 metallic for metallic threads, 80/12 topstitching
- Other materials: notions as called for on the pattern envelope, darning foot

INSTRUCTIONS

1. Prewash or dry-clean the interfacing and fashion fabrics according to the manufacturer's instructions.

2. From the lining, cut the jacket pieces as instructed on the pattern guide sheet. From the interfacing, cut the front and back pieces 1" larger than the pattern pieces. Also cut 1 left and 1 right sleeve 1" larger than the pattern piece. With a pencil, mark the straight of grain on the resin side of all of the interfacing pieces. If you are working with a 22"-wide interfacing, refer to "Interfacings" on page 11 to join 2 pieces so that they are large enough to fit the back of the jacket pattern.

3. Cut the patchwork fabrics parallel to the selvage in 3", 4", and 5" strips. Crosscut the strips into squares and rectangles, 3" x 3", 3" x 4", 4" x 4", 2" x 5", 3" x 5", and so forth. The size of the cut pieces is dependent upon the size of the garment being created. Cut smaller pieces for smaller garments and larger pieces for larger garments. Separate the pieces into piles by color.

4. Following the grain-line markings as a placement guide, randomly position the wrong side of the squares and rectangles onto the resin side of each interfacing piece, butting the edges. When the piece is covered and you are satisfied with the placement, follow the interfacing manufacturer's instructions to fuse the pieces in place. If your fabric selection includes napped fabrics, temporarily remove them from their position on the vest. Fuse the remaining pieces in place. Be sure to use a cool iron with sheer fabrics. Then spray the napped fabrics with spray adhesive and reposition them on the vest.

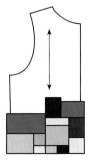

5. Refer to "Machine Setup and Stitching Techniques" on page 14 to set up the machine for free-motion stitching. Insert the topstitching needle into the machine. Referring to "Sewing with Twin and Triple Needles" on page 16, thread the needle with the 2 all-purpose threads selected for sealing the patch edges. Wind the bobbin with all-purpose or bobbin thread.

 Using leftover interfacing, make a patchwork sample large enough to use all the different fabrics. Use this sample to decide which thread is most flattering to the patchwork, to check tension, to try out different embellishments, and to make buttonholes.

6. Using an irregular, side-to-side zigzag motion, make a ⅛"- to ¼"-wide irregular straight stitch along the edges of each square. Stitch all of the horizontal edges first, then the vertical edges. Stitch in place to lock off threads when necessary.

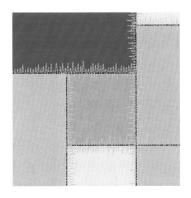

 If there are tiny gaps where the fabrics butt together, fill these areas with a couple of rows of straight stitching. Then cover the straight stitches with side-to-side stitching.

7. Press the pieces with steam to eliminate any puckering.

8. If desired, embellish the pieces with thread, ribbons, and cords. Refer to "Threadwork and Couching" on page 72 for additional information.

9. Lay the appropriate pattern on each piece. Cut out each piece along the pattern edges.

10. Finish the jacket as indicated in the pattern instructions. Topstitch the jacket edges.

Twin-Needle Pintucking

In this technique, rows of tiny mock tucks are created with a twin needle and a pintucking foot. Several variables play a part in forming the raised pintuck, however. The threads used in the needle and bobbin, the fabric weave and weight, and the top and bobbin tension can create distinctly different results on the finished product.

To better understand the process, let's discuss how the stitch is formed. The twin needle forms two rows of stitching on the fabric surface. Turn the fabric over and you can see that the bobbin thread zigzags back and forth between the rows on the underside of the fabric. If you set the machine for a balanced tension and used this technique, chances are your stitches would look like two ordinary rows of stitching. But, if either the top tension or bobbin tension is tightened, the rows of stitching will pull together, creating pintucks.

While there is only one way to tighten the top tension, there are a couple of ways to adjust the bobbin tension for this method. In addition to tightening the bobbin screw to adjust the bobbin tension (see page 13), the tension on some removable bobbin cases can also be tightened by threading the bobbin thread through the hole in the bobbin finger.

The type of fabric also plays a part in how well the tucks stand up. Lighter fabric tucks very easily, but heavier fabric, like denim, needs more tension changes. Stitch length also affects how the pintuck appears. A longer stitch creates a softer, flatter tuck and a short stitch creates a more rigid tuck. Experiment to see what works best for you.

This technique usually does not require extra yardage unless concentrated rows of pintucks are stitched, but it does require some additional knowledge about the supplies needed to form satisfactory pintucks. If you are sewing multiple rows of pintucks, you will need a pintucking foot to ensure evenly spaced rows. Pintucking feet are available with 3, 5, 7, and 9 grooves for use with different types of fabrics. The 3-groove foot is for heavier fabrics; the 5-groove is best for medium- to lightweight fabrics, and the 7- and 9-groove feet are for very fine fabrics. After the first row is stitched, place the tuck under one of the grooves in the foot and stitch the next row. Repeat for as many rows as desired. If you are stitching one row, an open-toe appliqué foot is adequate.

You will also need a twin needle. For general information on twin needles, refer to "Sewing with Twin and Triple Needles" on page 16. To choose the correct-size twin needle for your pintucking foot, turn the foot over and place the needles between 2 grooves. If they fit easily, then the needles are the correct distance apart for that foot. If the needles spread apart, then the space between the needles is not adequate for that foot. Select a twin needle with more distance between the needles, or a foot with narrower grooves.

For pintucking, set up the sewing machine for regular sewing. Attach the pintucking foot and insert the appropriate size twin needle. Refer to "Sewing with Twin and Triple Needles" on page 16 to thread the top with two spools of thread. Set the stitch length according to the fabric choice and the look desired.

Finally, prewash fabrics when possible. If a fabric needs to be stabilized, do it after the pintucks are stitched. If it is done before, the tucks will not stand up as much.

Pintuck Surprise

*Solid-color fabric showcases the elegance of simple,
random lines of pintucks. Finished with twisted braid
in a matching color, this versatile vest can be worn
with jeans or dressed up for a night out on the town.*

MATERIALS

- Any style of vest pattern. Use a pattern with minimum seams for your first project.

- Solid-color cotton or linen for the vest fashion fabric. To determine the yardage needed, do a mock layout with the front and back pieces. Because this vest is lined to the edge, ignore any facing pieces that may be called for in the pattern.

- Coordinating lining fabric. Determine the yardage in the same manner as for the fashion fabric.

- Fusible woven interfacing. To determine the yardage needed, do a mock layout with the vest pattern pieces, ignoring any facing pieces that may be called for in the pattern. If you are working with a 22"-wide interfacing, refer to "Interfacings" on page 11.

- Threads: all-purpose for construction in a color to match fashion fabric, your choice for the pintucks in a color to match fashion fabric, 2 skeins of #5 pearl cotton in a color to match fashion fabric for making twisted braid, invisible monofilament

- Needles: universal in a size appropriate for the fabric weight for construction of garment and stitching with invisible thread, 2.5/80 twin needle for pintucks

- Other materials: 5-groove pintuck foot; thread-twisting tool, such as The Spinster described on page 104, for making edge braid; buttons as called for on the pattern envelope

INSTRUCTIONS

1. Prewash or dry-clean the fabrics and interfacing according to the manufacturer's instructions.
2. From the fashion fabric, lining, and interfacing, cut the vest pieces. Because this vest is lined to the edges, ignore any facing pieces that may be called for in the pattern. If you are working with a 22"-wide interfacing, refer to "Interfacings" on page 11 to join 2 pieces so that they are large enough to fit the vest back pattern.
3. Refer to "Sewing with Twin and Triple Needles" on page 16 to set up the machine for twin-needle stitching. Use your desired thread in the needle and bobbin. After you make test samples and determine that the stitch length and tension are satisfactory, randomly stitch gently curving lines on each piece. Sew slowly and keep a slight tension on the fabric to lessen distortion problems. Sharp curves tend to distort the fabric so keep the curves very gradual.

 An odd number of pintuck lines creates a more pleasing visual effect than an even number of lines.

4. Press the pintucked pieces from the wrong side. Follow the manufacturer's instructions to fuse the corresponding interfacing piece to the wrong side of each pintucked piece.
5. Follow the pattern instructions to stitch the vest together at the shoulder seams. Refer to "Easy Vest Lining" on page 109 to assemble the lining and line the vest, leaving a 1" to 1½" opening at the neck and back lower edges.
6. Follow the pattern instructions to stitch the buttonholes in the vest right front.
7. Using the pearl cotton and a thread-twisting tool, refer to "Making Spinster Braid" on page 104 to make the braids, and "Mock Piping" on page 103 to apply it to the vest front edges with invisible thread.
8. Position the buttons on the vest left front to correspond with the buttonhole placement, and sew the buttons to the vest.

Quick-and-Easy Twisted Tucks

This fabric manipulation method involves using the lines of a plaid or stripe fabric to make tucks. Once the tucks are formed vertically, they are twisted or turned, and secured with a horizontal line of stitches.

Look for plaid fabric with stripes that are wide enough to fold in half and stitch into tucks. The most dramatic effect comes with a two-color stripe. Large plaids do not work as well as smaller plaid patterns. Even and uneven plaids can be used, but be aware that if you are working with an uneven plaid, the finished tucked fabric will need to be treated as a fabric with a nap and cut in one direction.

NOTE: I PREFER ¾"- TO 1¼"-WIDE STRIPS BECAUSE THEY CREATE ⅜" TO ⅝"-WIDE TUCKS.

To calculate the amount of fabric to purchase, look at the stripes that run from selvage edge to selvage edge. Decide which stripe will be tucked, measure its width, and count how many run across the width of the fabric. Multiply these numbers together, subtract that number from the fabric width, and you will have the amount of fabric left to work with after tucking. For example, a 60" wide fabric has 49 rows of a stripe that is ¾" wide (49 x ¾" = 36¾"; 60" − 36¾" = 23¼" of tucked fabric). Next, measure the length and width of the pattern pieces to determine the fabric needed.

Burgundy Twist

Glitzy and elegant fabrics make this vest a perfect choice for the holidays. Pintucked plaid taffeta takes the spotlight, with an embellished broomsticked velvet collar adding the perfect accent.

MATERIALS

- Vest pattern with collar and crossover front
- Approximately 1½ yds. of 60"-wide plaid taffeta for vest fronts. To determine the exact yardage, follow the instructions in "Quick and Easy Twisted Tucks" on page 65 to calculate the finished width of the pintucked fabric. Do a mock layout with the pattern pieces. Because the garment is lined to the edge, ignore any facing pieces that may be called for in the pattern.
- Broomsticked rayon velvet fabric for vest back and collar (see "Broomsticking" on page 52 and "Holiday Cheer" on page 53 for instructions to broomstick fabric). To determine the exact yardage, do a mock layout with the required pattern pieces. Use a 30" width for you calculations.
- Coordinating lining fabric. To determine the yardage needed, do a mock layout with the front, back, and collar pieces. Because this vest is lined to the edge, ignore any facing pieces that may be called for in the pattern.
- Fusible woven interfacing. To determine the yardage needed, do a mock layout with the vest front pattern pieces, ignoring any facing pieces that may be called for in the pattern.
- Threads: all-purpose for construction in a color to match fashion fabric, gold metallic for embellishing, 2 skeins each of #8 pearl cotton in 2 colors that match plaid fabric and a gold metallic cord for edge braid, invisible monofilament
- Needles: 80/12 universal for invisible thread and garment construction, 80/12 metallic for metallic thread
- Other materials: thread-twisting tool, such as The Spinster described on page 104, for making edge braid; buttons as called for on the pattern envelope

INSTRUCTIONS

1. Prewash the interfacing according to the manufacturer's instructions.
2. Cut the collar and back pieces from the broomsticked fabric and lining. Set the pieces aside.
3. To tuck the plaid fabric, begin by placing it wrong side up on an ironing board with one selvage edge parallel to the board, and the bulk of the fabric hanging over the front of the ironing board.

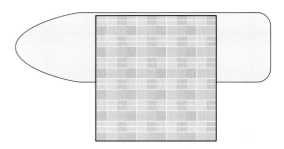

4. Press the first tuck by folding the selvage over to the wrong side and setting a crease in the selected stripe with a steam iron. Continue to crease all of the selected stripes in the same manner, with the creased tucks curling over the unpressed fabric and hanging over the front of the ironing board.

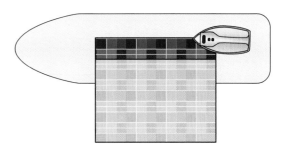

5. Refer to "Machine Setup and Stitching Techniques" on page 14 to set up the machine for regular sewing. Thread the needle and bobbin with all-purpose thread. Pin and stitch the length of the first tuck into place. Use the stripes as your stitching-line guide. Repeat until all of the tucks have been stitched. Press all of the tucks in one direction from the right side of the fabric; then press from the wrong

Create Your Own Collar

If your favorite crossover-front vest does not have a collar, adding your own is easy. All you need is a pencil and a piece of tracing paper large enough to accommodate the pattern.

1. Mark the center of the shoulder upper edge on the vest front pattern. Draw a gently curving line from the mark to the front point as shown.

2. Place the paper over the pattern and trace the design. Add a ¼" seam allowance to the curved edge and a ⅝" seam allowance to the remaining edges.

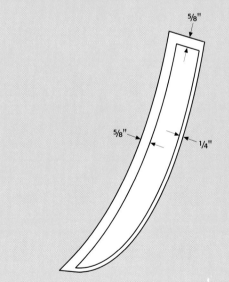

side to ensure that all of the seams are open and pressed flat.

6. Stitch across the tucks at the top and bottom edges of the fabric. To determine where the tucks will be turned, choose a horizontal stripe to use as a guide for stitching the twisted tucks in place. Experiment with different stripes until you find a stripe that achieves a pleasing look. Some stripes look better turned every 2" and other stripes look better turned every 3" to 4". Generally, a narrow stripe or tuck looks best if it is turned more often than a wider stripe or tuck. The bulk of the stripe also helps to make a decision of how often to turn it. Pin the tucks in place where they are to be turned, alternately twisting them in opposite directions.

7. Refer to "Machine Setup and Stitching Techniques" on page 14 to set up the machine for regular sewing. Insert the metallic needle into the machine. Thread the needle with gold metallic thread. Set up the machine for a straight or decorative stitch, and check the tension.

8. Stitching in the direction the tucks were pinned, stitch across the row of tucks. Use one of the plaid lines as a guide.

9. When all of the tucks are stitched, press the tucks in the direction they were stitched.

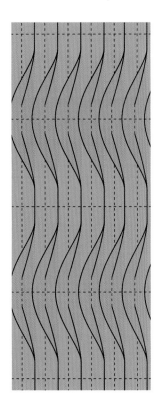

10. Using the same machine setup, straight stitch random rows of gently curving lines on the velvet collar and back pieces.

11. From the tucked fabric, interfacing, and lining, cut out the vest front pieces.

12. Follow the manufacturer's instructions to fuse the corresponding interfacing piece to the wrong side of each tucked piece.

13. Stitch the collar lining to the collar. Turn the collar to the right side and press. Using the 2 colors of pearl cotton and the gold metallic cord, refer to "Making Spinster Braid" on page 104 to make 2 Spinster braids. Using invisible thread, refer to "Mock Piping" on page 103 to stitch the braids to the finished collar curved edge, beginning at the shoulder edge and ending halfway down the collar. Coil up the remaining braid and pin it to the collar. Baste the collar to the vest right front at the shoulder and front edges. Follow the pattern instructions to stitch the front to the back at the shoulder seams.

14. Refer to "Easy Vest Lining" on page 109 to assemble the lining and line the vest, leaving a 1" to 1½" opening at the center back lower edge and left shoulder seam.

15. Follow the pattern instructions to stitch the buttonholes in the vest right front.

16. Using invisible thread, stitch the remaining braid to the collar, vest fronts, and lower back edges.

17. Position the buttons on the vest left front to correspond with the buttonhole placement, and sew the buttons to the vest.

Apply seam sealant to thread shanks and knots after attaching the buttons, and to buttonholes before cutting them open.

Fabric Manipulation
PHOTO GALLERY

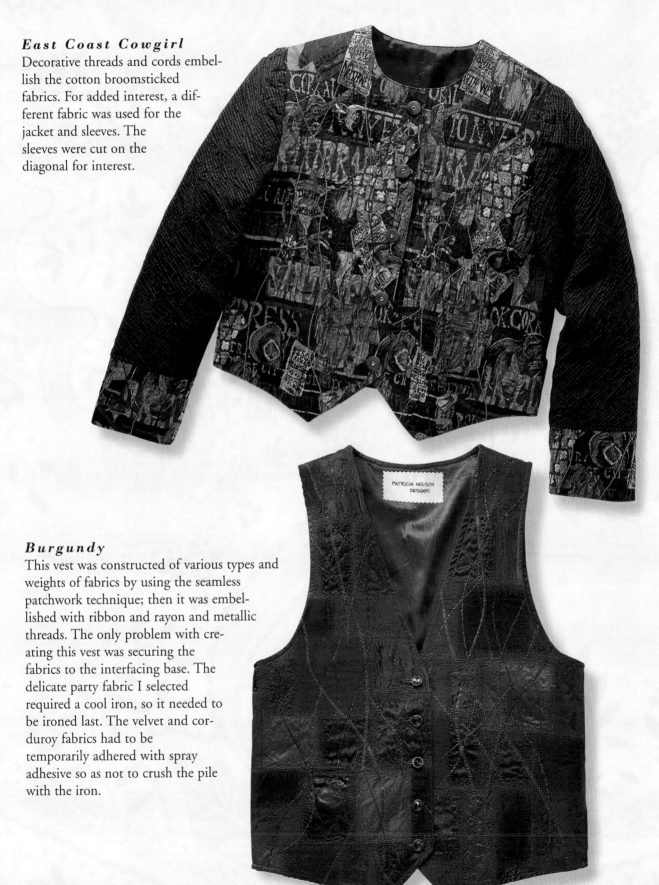

East Coast Cowgirl

Decorative threads and cords embellish the cotton broomsticked fabrics. For added interest, a different fabric was used for the jacket and sleeves. The sleeves were cut on the diagonal for interest.

Burgundy

This vest was constructed of various types and weights of fabrics by using the seamless patchwork technique; then it was embellished with ribbon and rayon and metallic threads. The only problem with creating this vest was securing the fabrics to the interfacing base. The delicate party fabric I selected required a cool iron, so it needed to be ironed last. The velvet and corduroy fabrics had to be temporarily adhered with spray adhesive so as not to crush the pile with the iron.

Evening Out

Spaced rows of pintucking form the border of the body and sleeves on this taffeta jacket, while crosshatch fills in the open areas. The pintucks were created with metallic thread, but because the jacket was interfaced before the pintucks were stitched, there was little dimension to the tucks.

Christmas Tucks

This holiday jacket was constructed with a plaid taffeta and a polyester fabric. To give texture and add color, the taffeta bodice was tucked along a stripe of the plaid, twisted, and stitched in place with invisible thread. The bodice bands and sleeves were machine trapuntoed with a metallic ribbon thread in a poinsettia motif. A stippling technique was then used with invisible thread on the bodice and sleeve bands. Free-motion stitching was used for channel quilting the upper sleeve with straight lines set closely together and the same invisible thread. The centers of the poinsettias were beaded. Finally, the black and gold braid was couched with invisible thread. Not shown are a coordinating vest, blouse, slacks, and belt.

Fabric Embellishments

Embellishing is the act of decorating fabric with assorted threads, braids, cords, or fabric. These decorations may be random or planned. In this chapter you learn to do threadwork, couching, bobbin work, machine appliqué, and machine embroidery.

Threadwork and Couching

The basic difference between threadwork and couching is that in threadwork the decorative thread can be placed in the needle and stitched to the fabric. Couching involves heavier cords and braids that are too thick to fit through the needle, so they are placed on the fabric and stitched in place to secure them.

Threadwork can be either a machine-guided or free-motion process. The stitching can vary from slightly lengthened straight stitches to a utility stitch, such as the triple stitch, to a decorative stitch, such as the feather stitch. Often threadwork serves as a great base for giving a plain fabric some texture, as shown in "Origami Patch Vest" (page 56) and "Poinsettias" (page 78). It also is great for embellishing broomsticked fabric. For examples, see "Evening Tango" (page 49) and "Holiday Cheer" (page 53).

Couching, a machine-guided process, involves placing a cord or braid on the surface of the fabric and zigzag stitching it in place. The effect can be simple or decorative, depending on the sewing threads and stitches used. An invisible thread lets the cord or braid stand on its own, while a contrasting rayon or metallic thread adds dimension. Use a decorative stitch and it will add even more dimension to the cord or thread. Adjust the stitch width so that the needle swing just misses piercing the ribbon or braid.

While you do not need to use a special presser foot, there are many available that make it easier to apply decorative threads. As shown in the photo at right, an embroidery foot (a) has a small hole in the front of the crossbar. Thread it with finer cords, such as pearl cotton, for couching work. A single large groove on the underside of the tricot foot (b) will accommodate pearls, beads,

and other bulky trims. The foot is placed over the pearls or braid and they are stitched in place with invisible thread and a zigzag stitch. Always use the hand wheel to make the first few stitches to ensure the zigzag stitch is wide enough to go over them. A braiding foot (c) has a hole in the top of the foot that serves as a guide for sewing down all sorts of braids, cords, and narrow ribbons. It also has a large groove on the underside to accommodate the extra thickness. The 3- and 5-groove cording feet, (d) and (e), are used to apply several colors of thinner threads or cords to create custom braid. A thread is inserted into each groove and the spring is closed over them to secure them. They are then secured to the fabric with a wide decorative or utility stitch.

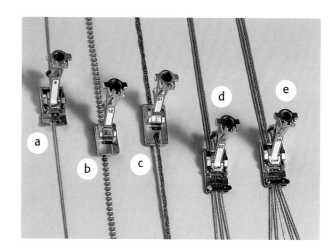

 Tip When couching different thicknesses of cords, sew the thickest ones last, especially if you are applying beads or pearls. Pearls and beads are easily broken if stitched over with another braid and pierced with a needle.

It's Always Greener

Take a plain-Jane fabric, use the broomstick technique, and embellish it with threadwork, couching, and decorative stitches. The result is anything but ordinary.

MATERIALS

- Vest pattern of your choice with front button closure
- Cotton fashion fabric, broomsticked and stabilized with interfacing as described in "Broomsticking" on page 52 and "Holiday Cheer" on page 53. To determine the yardage required, do a mock layout with the pattern pieces. Use a 30" width for your calculations. Because the vest is lined to the edges, ignore any facing pieces that may be called for in the pattern.
- Coordinating lining fabric. To determine the yardage needed, do a mock layout with the front and back pieces. Because

this vest is lined to the edge, ignore any facing pieces that may be called for in the pattern.

- Threads: all-purpose for construction, 3 coordinating colors of rayon for thread-work, invisible monofilament for couching braids, gold metallic, 2 skeins of #5 pearl cotton in a color to match fashion fabric for Spinster braid
- Needles: 80/12 universal for invisible thread and garment construction, 75/11 embroidery for rayon thread, tapestry or chenille for hand sewing
- Other materials: open-toe appliqué foot; couching/braiding foot; 3 yards of metallic braid for leaf design; thread-twisting tool, such as The Spinster described on page 104, for making edge braid; buttons as called for on the pattern envelope; seam sealant

INSTRUCTIONS

1. Prewash or dry-clean the lining fabric according to the manufacturer's instructions.
2. From the broomsticked fabric and lining, cut the vest pieces.
3. Refer to "Machine Setup and Stitching Techniques" on page 14 to set up the machine for regular sewing. Attach the open-toe appliqué foot. Insert the embroidery needle. Thread the needle with one of the colors of rayon thread, and wind the bobbin with all-purpose thread.
4. After you make test samples and determine that the stitch length and tension are satisfactory, stitch 2 to 3 vertical rows of gently curving lines on the vest fronts and 5 rows on the vest back. Repeat with the remaining rayon threads.

5. Insert the universal needle. Attach the couching/braiding foot. Thread the machine with invisible thread. Set the stitch for a balanced, narrow zigzag that just clears the braid. Insert the braid into the foot.

6. After you make test samples and determine that the stitch length and tension are satisfactory, stitch the leaf design on both fronts and the back. Beginning at the center of the shoulder upper edge, stitch a gently curved line for about 5". With the needle in the fabric, pivot back toward the couched braid. Stitch a curved line back toward the braid to create a leaf. At the point where the braid crosses the original line, insert the needle and pivot again in the direction of the vest lower edge. Stitch for about 2" to 3" past the previous leaf; then pivot in the opposite direction and repeat the leaf making process. Continue to repeat the process until the branch is the desired length, leaving a 4" to 5" thread tail at the end.

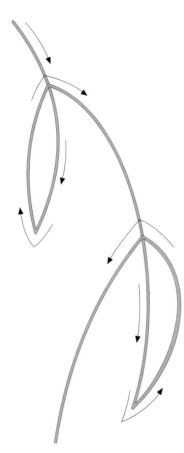

 Place the needle on the side of the braid in the direction you wish to turn. For example, if you want to turn right, place the needle on the right side of the braid and pivot to the right.

7. Thread the braid end through the eye of the tapestry or chenille needle. Insert the needle into the fabric close to the last couched stitch, and pull it through to the back of the fabric. Knot the end close to the surface of the fabric. Trim the thread tail to 1". Secure with seam sealant.

8. Steam-press each piece from both sides.

9. Thread the needle with one of the rayon thread colors in the needle and gold metallic thread in the bobbin. Loosen the top tension slightly so bits of the bobbin thread show on the right side. Set the machine for a preprogrammed star design and randomly stitch stars to the vest pieces, or create your own stitching design, such as a stitch-in-place zigzag, to create a small, raised dot. Leave thread tails at the end of each star. Pull the thread tails to the vest wrong side and knot the ends together to secure.

10. Follow the pattern instructions to stitch the front to the back at the shoulder seams. Refer to "Easy Vest Lining" on page 109 to assemble the lining and line the vest, leaving a 1" to 1½" opening at the center back neckline and lower edges. Using the pearl cotton, refer to "Making Spinster Braid" on page 104 to make Spinster braids. Refer to "Mock Piping" on page 103 to stitch the braid to the vest front and lower edges with invisible thread, forming Sew-As-You-Go loop closures on the vest right front as instructed in "Button Loop Closures" on page 105.

11. Position the buttons on the vest left front to correspond with the loop closure placement, and sew the buttons to the vest.

Bobbinwork

Bobbinwork, also known as the cable stitch, is another method for sewing thicker threads to fabric. In this method, however, the decorative thread is wound on the bobbin and the design is sewn with the wrong side of the work facing up. Because the bobbin tension will need adjusting, it is a good idea to purchase an extra bobbin case if you have a machine with a removable bobbin case. Check your owner's manual for instructions on adjusting the tension if you own a machine with a drop-in bobbin case.

Tip When removing thicker threads from the bobbin case, clip the thread at the bobbin case. Do not pull the thread through the bobbin spring because it can leave thread particles, which can affect the tension later.

Bobbinwork can be a machine-guided or free-motion process. Refer to "Machine Setup and Stitching Techniques" on page 14 for instructions on setting up your machine for either of these stitching techniques.

Copycat Vest

Take the design motif from a purchased blouse and use it to create a one-of-a-kind vest. The subtle tone-on-tone embellishment is sure to enhance an otherwise plain garment.

MATERIALS

- Purchased blouse with a motif suitable to use for the vest design embellishment
- Vest pattern of your choice
- Fashion fabric. To determine the yardage needed, do a mock layout with the front and back pieces. Because the vest is lined to the edge, ignore any facing pieces that may be called for in the pattern.
- Coordinating lining fabric. Determine the yardage in the same manner as for the fashion fabric.
- Fusible woven interfacing. To determine the yardage needed, do a mock layout with the vest pattern pieces, ignoring any facing pieces that may be called for in the pattern. If you are working with a 22"-wide interfacing, refer to "Interfacings" on page 11.
- Threads: all-purpose in a color to match fashion fabric, 5 skeins of #5 pearl cotton in a color to match fashion fabric
- Needles: 80/12 universal for machine sewing, tapestry or chenille for hand sewing
- Other materials: tracing paper, light box, darning foot, buttons as called for on the pattern envelope, marking tool, embroidery hoop.

INSTRUCTIONS

1. From the fashion fabric, lining, and interfacing, cut the vest pieces. Because this vest is lined to the edges, ignore any facing pieces that may be called for in the pattern. If you are working with a 22"-wide interfacing, refer to "Interfacings" on page 11 to join 2 pieces so that they are large enough to fit the vest back pattern.
2. Transfer the desired motif from the purchased blouse onto tracing paper. Use a light box to transfer the motif to the nonresin side of the

interfacing pieces, placing the motif as desired on each piece. Avoid tracing the motifs in the seam allowance.

3. Follow the manufacturer's directions to fuse the interfacing to the wrong side of the coordinating fashion fabric pieces.
4. Refer to "Machine Setup and Stitching Techniques" on page 14 to set up the machine for free-motion stitching. Thread the needle with matching all-purpose thread. Machine wind the bobbin with pearl cotton, hand guiding the thread so the bobbin fills evenly. Referring to "Understanding Tension" on page 13, place the bobbin into the bobbin case and adjust the tension so that the thread pulls through it smoothly with some tension.
5. After you make test samples and determine that the tension is satisfactory, hoop the fabric so that the fashion fabric is right side down against the throat plate. Take a stitch to pull the pearl cotton to the top. Holding both threads, begin stitching. Follow the designs marked on the interfacing to stitch the motifs on each piece. Keep the stitches even. After each motif has been stitched, leave a 3" tail and thread the end of the pearl cotton through the eye of the tapestry needle; pull it through to the back of the fabric. Knot the ends close to the surface of the fabric. Trim the tails to 1".

Tip Hoop the fabric with a 6"–8" embroidery hoop if fabric distortion occurs.

6. Follow the pattern instructions to stitch the front to the back at the shoulder seams. Refer to "Easy Vest Lining" on page 109 to assemble the lining and line the vest.
7. Follow the pattern instructions to make the buttonholes and attach the buttons.

Machine Appliqué

Appliqué is a method of applying fabric pieces as decorative designs to a background fabric. Fused, soft-touch fused, and invisible machine appliqué with a twist are covered in this section.

Fused Appliqué

Fused appliqué is probably the quickest appliqué method. In this method, paper-backed fusible web is fused to the wrong side of the appliqué fabric. The appliqué is cut out, the paper backing is removed from the appliqué, and then the motif is fused to the garment. Because the edges of the motif are unfinished and susceptible to raveling, the raw edges must be sealed. There are several ways to seal the edges, including, but not limited to, traditional satin stitch, blanket stitch, side-to-side free-motion stitching, and six to eight rows of free-motion stitching around the raw edges.

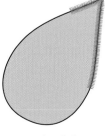

Satin stitch

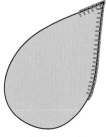

Blanket stitch

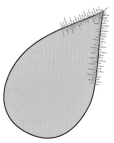

Side-to-side
free-motion stitching

6–8 rows of
free-motion stitching
around raw edge

Poinsettias

Try your hand at a simple alteration to make this vest from two fabrics. Embellished with just the right amount of metallic thread, the vest front features appliqué motifs taken from the vest lining fabric.

PATRICIA NELSON
DESIGNS

MATERIALS

- Vest pattern of your choice
- Solid-color cotton fabric for the vest upper section. To determine the yardage required, make the pattern alterations as described in step 2 of the instructions, then do a mock layout with the pattern piece and the appropriate fabric.
- Complementary print fabric for the vest lower section. To determine the yardage required, make the pattern alterations as described in step 2 of the instructions, then do a mock layout with the pattern piece and the appropriate fabric.
- Cotton fabric for lining and appliqués. Select a fabric with a distinguishable motif suitable for the appliqués on the vest front. To determine the yardage, do a mock layout with the vest front and back pieces; then add ½ yard extra for the appliqués. Because the garment is lined to the edge, ignore any facing pieces that may be called for in the pattern.
- Fusible woven interfacing. To determine the yardage needed, do a mock layout with the vest pattern pieces, ignoring any facing pieces that may be called for in the pattern. If you are working with a 22"-wide interfacing, refer to "Interfacings" on page 11.
- Threads: all-purpose for construction in a color to match vest solid-color fabric, 3 colors of metallic thread for embellishing, rayon in colors to match appliqués
- Needles: 80/12 universal for construction, 80/12 metallic for metallic threads, 75/11 embroidery for rayon thread
- Other materials: 1 yd. of paper-backed fusible web, darning foot, purchased braid for the vest edges, pattern tracing paper, other notions as called for on the pattern envelope

INSTRUCTIONS

1. Prewash or dry-clean the fashion fabric, interfacing, and lining according to the manufacturer's instructions.

2. To make the pattern alterations, trace the vest front and a whole back onto pattern tracing paper and cut them out. Draw a gently curving line from side to side on the back tracing paper pattern, beginning and ending at the same place on each side seam. Place the front tracing paper pattern next to the marked back pattern. Beginning at the same place on the side seam, draw a gently curving line from side to side on the front pattern. Label each section. Cut the patterns apart on the drawn line. Use these pieces to calculate the yardage for the vest.

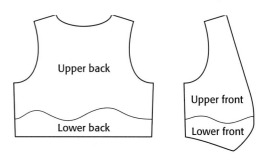

3. Using the original tissue patterns, cut the vest pieces from interfacing and lining. If you are working with a 22"-wide interfacing, refer to "Interfacings" on page 11 to join 2 pieces so that they are large enough to fit the vest back pattern.

4. Using the tracing paper patterns, cut the upper fronts and upper back from the solid-color fabric. Cut the lower fronts and lower back from the complementary fabric.

5. Place the front interfacing pieces on the ironing board, resin side up. Place the vest upper and lower front pieces, wrong sides down, over the interfacing pieces. Butt the upper and

lower sections together. Follow the manufacturer's instructions to fuse the pieces to the interfacing. Repeat for the back pieces.

6. Refer to "Machine Setup and Stitching Techniques" on page 14 to set up the machine for regular sewing. Insert the metallic needle. Thread the machine with one of the metallic threads in the needle, and wind the bobbin with all-purpose thread in a color to match the solid-color fabric.

7. After you make test samples and determine that the stitch length and tension are satisfactory, stitch meandering lines on the upper section of each piece. Repeat with the remaining metallic thread colors.

8. Follow the manufacturer's instructions to apply fusible web to the wrong side of the appliqué fabric. Cut 2 motifs from the fabric. Remove the paper backing and fuse the motifs to the front pieces as shown.

9. Refer to "Machine Setup and Stitching Techniques" on page 14 to set up the machine for free-motion stitching. Thread the needle with one of the metallic thread colors. After you make test samples and determine that the tension is satisfactory, use

an irregular, side-to-side zigzag motion (see page 78) to straight stitch along the edge where the upper and lower sections meet. As you come to the appliqué, lock off the stitches, raise the needle out of the fabric, lift the presser foot, and drag the thread to the other side of the appliqué and begin stitching again. Go over the stitches with one of the remaining colors of metallic thread.

10. Insert the embroidery needle into the machine. Thread the machine with rayon thread to match the appliqué. After you make test samples and determine that the tension is satisfactory, use an irregular, side-to-side zigzag motion to straight stitch over the appliqué raw edges. Change thread colors as desired.

11. Press the finished pieces. Follow the pattern instructions to stitch the fronts to the back at the shoulder seams. Refer to "Easy Vest Lining" on page 109 to assemble the lining and line the vest, leaving a 1" to 1½" opening at the center back neckline.

12. Follow the pattern instructions to stitch the buttonholes in the vest right front.

13. Refer to "Mock Piping" on page 103 to stitch the purchased braid to the vest fronts and back edges.

14. Position the buttons on the vest left front to correspond with the buttonhole placement, and sew the buttons to the vest.

Soft-Touch Appliqué

Created by Deb Wagner, this technique is similar to fused appliqué but creates a softer finish because the fusible web is only applied to the appliqué edges rather than the entire motif. Use any of the stitches shown on page 78 to seal the edges.

Tonal Flowers

Turn a basic sweatshirt cardigan into a stylish wardrobe addition with subtle, tone-on-tone appliqués. A free-motion straight stitch finishes the edges of the soft-touch appliqués.

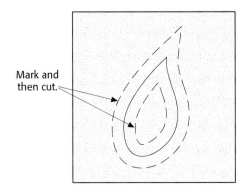

MATERIALS

- Purchased sweatshirt cardigan
- Small amount of polyester satin fabric scraps in a color to match cardigan for appliqués
- Threads: all-purpose in a color to match appliqués, rayon in a color to match appliqués
- 75/11 embroidery needle
- Other materials: ½ yard of paper-backed fusible web, darning foot, several sheets of typing paper or tear-away stabilizer

INSTRUCTIONS

1. Prewash the garment and appliqué fabrics.
2. Trace the motifs on page 82 onto the paper side of the fusible web. Mark ¼" on each side of the lines. Using the lines on the inside and outside of the original line, cut out the design.

Mark and then cut.

3. Follow the manufacturer's instructions to fuse the webbing shapes to the wrong side of the appliqué fabric. Cut out the motifs on the original design line.

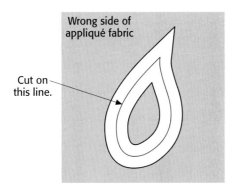

Wrong side of appliqué fabric

Cut on this line.

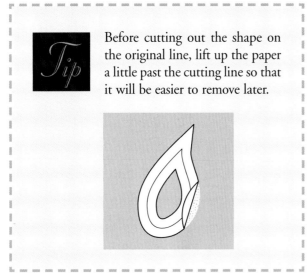

Tip

Before cutting out the shape on the original line, lift up the paper a little past the cutting line so that it will be easier to remove later.

4. Remove the paper backing. Follow the manufacturer's instructions to fuse the appliqués to the garment, referring to the photo for placement.

5. Refer to "Machine Setup and Stitching Techniques" on page 14 to set up the machine for free-motion stitching. Insert the embroidery needle. Thread the machine with the rayon thread and wind the bobbin with all-purpose thread. Test the stitch tension on a double layer of appliqué fabric.

6. Place 2 layers of typing paper or stabilizer under the motifs. Using a free-motion straight stitch, stitch around each motif 6 to 8 times to cover the raw edge. Place the first row of stitches ⅛" from the motif raw edge.

7. Tear away the typing paper or stabilizer.

Tonal Flowers
Patterns

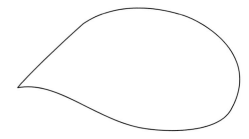

Invisible Machine Appliqué with a Twist

This technique is a combination of freezer-paper appliqué and a machine adaptation of Nancy Pearson's twisted-fabric hand-appliqué method. The end result makes the fabric look as if it were actually turned.

Calla Lilies

Beautiful calla lilies add elegance and richness to a simple, unstructured jacket that you make or purchase. Looking almost lifelike, the illusion is easy to replicate with subtle changes in color and the machine appliqué-with-a-twist technique.

MATERIALS

- Unstructured, button-front jacket pattern of your choice
- Lightweight cotton fabric. To determine the yardage needed, do a mock layout with the jacket pieces, ignoring any facing pieces called for in the pattern.
- Coordinating lining fabric. Determine the yardage in the same manner as for the fashion fabric.
- Cotton fabrics for the appliqués: ¼ yard green for the flower stem, scraps of 2 medium pinks and a dark pink for the flowers, scrap of yellow for the spikes
- Fusible tricot interfacing. To determine the yardage needed, do a mock layout with the jacket pattern pieces, ignoring any facing pieces that may be called for in

the pattern. If you are working with a 22"-wide interfacing, refer to "Interfacings" on page 11.

- Threads: all-purpose for construction, rayon in 5 colors to match appliqué fabrics for embellishing jacket fabric; invisible monofilament for securing appliqués
- Needles: 80/12 universal for invisible thread and garment construction, 75/11 embroidery for rayon threads
- Other materials: walking foot, open-toe appliqué foot, 4" embroidery scissors, tracing paper, freezer paper, water-soluble gluestick, several sheets of typing paper, chalk pencil, other notions as called for on the pattern envelope

INSTRUCTIONS

1. Prewash or dry-clean the fashion fabric, interfacing, and lining according to the manufacturer's instructions.

2. From the fashion fabric, lining, and interfacing, cut the jacket pieces, ignoring any facing pieces that may be called for in the pattern. If you are working with a 22"-wide interfacing, refer to "Interfacings" on page 11 to join 2 pieces so that they are large enough to fit the jacket back pattern.

3. Follow the manufacturer's instructions to fuse the interfacing pieces to the wrong side of the corresponding fashion fabric pieces.

4. Refer to "Machine Setup and Stitching Techniques" on page 14 to set up the machine for machine-guided sewing. Insert the embroidery needle into the machine. Thread the needle with one of the colors of rayon thread, and wind the bobbin with all-purpose thread. After you make test samples and determine that the stitch length and tension are satisfactory, stitch 3 rows of gently curving lines on the front pieces and 5 to 6 rows on the back. Repeat with the remaining 4 colors. Please note that the walking foot minimizes puckering when stitching on lightweight fabrics.

5. Trace 2 small calla lilies, 1 large calla lily, and 3 spike appliqués on page 87 onto tracing paper. Be sure to transfer the slash marks, *X*s, and numbers. Areas marked with a slash and an *X* denote interlocking pieces. The slash marks indicate where the fabric seam allowances are clipped, and the *X* marks indicate where the seam allowances are *not* to be glued. This creates fabric tags on each piece, which allow them to be interlocked and create a natural dimensional-looking flower.

Point Well Taken

Creating a sharp point is tricky. Follow these instructions for perfect points.

1. Trim the seam allowance across the point to about ⅛".

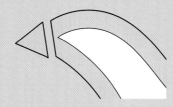

2. Fold the seam allowance over the point and then fold either side of the point on top. Use additional glue if needed.

Fold tip.

Fold over one edge.   Fold over second edge.

No-Bump Edges

If your edges aren't smooth, it could be caused by a tuck in the seam allowance. Lift up the seam allowance and redistribute the fabric. Sometimes the seam allowance is too wide and will cause this problem also. Try trimming it a bit or take V-shaped notches out of it. Also check to see if the pattern edge is smooth.

6. Trace over the design lines on the reverse side of the tracing paper to make a mirror image of the design. Use the mirror-image designs to trace the designs onto the paper side of freezer paper. Carefully transfer all of the markings to the freezer-paper patterns.

7. Cut the flower patterns apart along the solid lines to separate each section. Be careful to maintain smooth edges when cutting.

 When cutting apart each section, turn the paper with your hand instead of moving the scissors around the piece.

8. Lay the shiny side of the freezer-paper patterns on the wrong side of the appropriate appliqué fabrics. Grain line does not matter. Set your iron for a temperature suitable for the appliqué fabrics. With the heated dry iron, press the appliqués in place for 5 to 10 seconds.

9. Cut out the appliqué piece, leaving $\frac{3}{16}$" around the outer edges for seam allowances. Clip concave curves on the bias. Where there is a slash mark on the pattern, clip the seam allowance close to, but not through, the freezer paper.

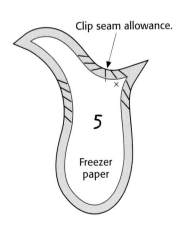

Clip seam allowance.

Freezer paper

10. Apply gluestick to the seam allowances, except on seam allowances where there is an X on the pattern, and ¼" onto the freezer-paper pattern. Work on a piece of typing paper to keep your work surface clean.

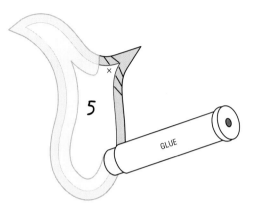

GLUE

11. Using your thumb and forefinger, roll the glued seam allowances over the pattern edges. Press each finished piece, glue side down, on a clean piece of paper and run your finger around the edge. This helps to seal the edges and check for smooth edges. Glue one piece at a time.

12. Using the original pattern on page 87 as a guide, interlock the flower pieces.

13. Place the flower appliqués on the jacket right front as desired. Determine the stem positions and lightly mark their placement lines with a chalk pencil.

14. To make the stems, cut 1"-wide bias strips from the green fabric. Stitch strips together if necessary to create the desired length. Press each strip in half lengthwise, wrong sides together. Place the stem raw edges on the marked lines on the jacket right front.

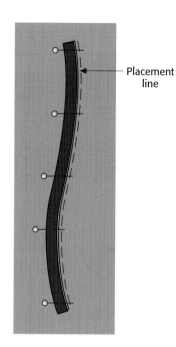

Placement line

15. Refer to "Machine Setup and Stitching Techniques" on page 14 to set up the machine for regular sewing. Using all-purpose thread in the needle and bobbin, straight stitch ⅛" from each stem raw edge. The width to stitch from the raw edge varies and depends on how wide you desire the finished stem to be.

16. Set the machine for a narrow, short zigzag stitch. Attach the open-toe appliqué foot. Thread the needle with invisible thread. After you make test samples and determine that the stitch length and tension are satisfactory, roll the stem folded edge over the stitched edge. Pin, and then stitch the folded edge in place, just catching 2 to 3 threads of the stem with one swing of the zigzag stitch. The other swing of the zigzag stitch should fall close to the appliqué fold. The stitch length should be about ⅛".

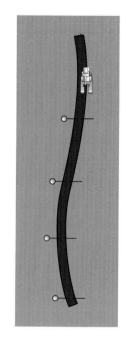

17. Position the flower appliqués over the stem ends. Pin them in place with 2 pins for each piece. Zigzag stitch along the edges in the same manner as the stems. To lock the thread where you started, stitch over the beginning zigzag stitches with ¼" of very short, straight stitches in the jacket fabric.

18. Working on the wrong side of the appliquéd piece, cut away the fabric behind each freezer-paper piece (leave the stems intact), leaving a ¼" seam allowance (a). Wet the freezer-paper patterns with water and let them

Wrong side of fabric

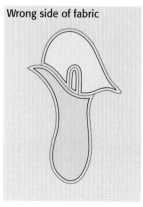

(a)

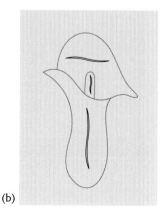

(b)

stand for 10 to 15 minutes. Remove the freezer paper. Another option for removing the freezer-paper patterns is to make a slit on the fabric wrong side behind the appliqué (b). Follow the same wetting procedure to remove the paper. If the slit is cut too big and the fabric hangs, seal the opening with a small piece of fusible interfacing.

19. Gently wash the appliquéd piece to remove excess glue, then assemble the jacket following the pattern instructions. If desired, refer to "Button Loop Closures" on page 105 to make the fabric button loops, and stitch the buttons to the jacket left front.

20. Topstitch the jacket outer edges.

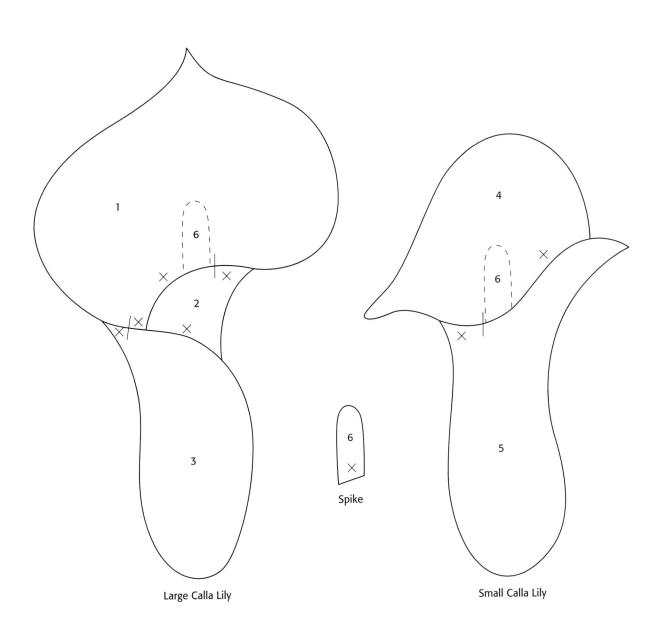

Large Calla Lily

Spike

Small Calla Lily

Calla Lilies
Patterns

Machine Embroidery

Machine embroidery, also known as thread painting or thread sketching, is a technique that allows the sewer to draw pictures or designs on fabric with thread by using a free-motion and/or a machine-guided setup and an embroidery hoop.

For free-motion embroidery, use a straight stitch rather than a zigzag stitch. It is less bulky, causes less distortion, and allows for interesting color variations in the thread. If possible, interface garment pieces before embroidering them. There are instances when this can't be done because the hoop will leave a permanent mark in some interfaced fabric. Check your fabric before starting to be sure the hoop marks can be removed both with and without interfacing.

Plaid Twist

Make your own textured fabric by using a small zigzag stitch to form slubs in the plaid design of this go-everywhere vest. Decorative machine stitching encloses the plaid design to create a striking border, while a purchased braid finishes the edges.

MATERIALS

- Lined vest pattern of your choice with a plain front, straight lower edge, and front button closure
- Solid-color fashion fabric. To determine the yardage needed, do a mock layout with the front and back pieces. Because this vest is lined to the edge, ignore any facing pieces that may be called for in the pattern.
- Coordinating lining fabric. Determine the yardage in the same manner as for the fashion fabric.
- Fusible woven interfacing. To determine the yardage needed, do a mock layout with the vest pattern pieces, ignoring any facing pieces that may be called for in the pattern. If you are working with a 22"-wide interfacing, refer to "Interfacings" on page 11.
- Threads: all-purpose for construction, 2–3 spools of 35-weight variegated rayon twist for embroidery, bobbin thread, invisible monofilament
- Needles: 80/12 universal for invisible thread and garment construction, 75/11 embroidery for rayon thread
- Other materials: open-toe appliqué foot, chalk wheel, purchased braid in yardage slightly longer than vest outer edge measurement, buttons as called for on the pattern envelope

INSTRUCTIONS

1. Prewash or dry-clean the fashion fabric, interfacing, and lining according to the manufacturer's instructions.
2. From the fashion fabric, lining, and interfacing, cut the vest pieces. Because this vest is lined to the edges, ignore any facing pieces that may be called for in the pattern. If you

Use the same stitch for the inner and outer border lines and a different stitch for the center line.

are working with a 22"-wide interfacing, refer to "Interfacings" on page 11 to join 2 pieces so that they are large enough to fit the vest back pattern.

3. Follow the manufacturer's instructions to fuse the interfacing pieces to the wrong side of the corresponding fashion fabric pieces.
4. With fabric scraps, design a border pattern approximately 1" wide. Use the decorative and utility stitches available on your machine. Or, if your machine does not have decorative options, try rows of straight stitches alternated with rows of different zigzag stitch widths.

NOTE: A WIDER BORDER, APPROXIMATELY 1½" TO 2" WIDE, IS APPROPRIATE FOR A JACKET.

5. Using the chalk wheel, draw the outside border line ¾" from the outside edges of the vest on the front and back pieces. Do not mark the armhole edges. Draw the second line (center border line) ½" from the first line. Draw the inner border line ½" from the center border line. If your border design is more than 1" wide, adjust the lines accordingly.

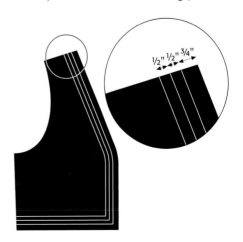

6. Mark the vertical plaid guidelines. On each piece, mark the first vertical line parallel to the center front and ½" from the inner border line. Draw the next line 1½" away from the first line. Continue marking lines 1½" from the previous line until the blank areas between the border lines are covered.

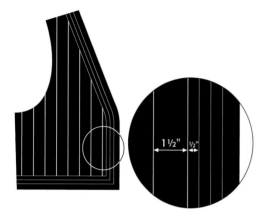

7. Mark the horizontal plaid guidelines. On each piece, mark the first line parallel to and ½" from the bottom of the vest. Draw in the remaining horizontal lines 1½" apart in the same manner as the vertical lines.

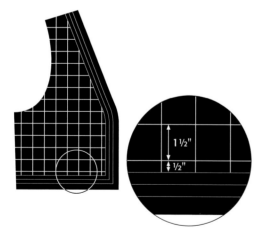

8. Refer to "Machine Setup and Stitching Techniques" on page 14 to set up the machine for regular sewing. Attach the open-toe appliqué foot. Insert the embroidery needle. Thread the needle with the rayon thread and wind the bobbin with bobbin thread or all-purpose thread, whichever will give the desired result. If you have a machine that switches back and forth between a straight and zigzag stitch, set the straight stitch for a stitch length between 2.5 and 3. Set the zigzag stitch for a stitch width between 1 and 1.25 and a stitch length of .5 so that the stitch looks like a slub. If your machine does not have a 2-stitch memory, try creating the stitch with your zigzag stitch only. Set the width at 0 and the length at 2.5. Stitch for about ½" to 1". Widen the stitch to 1 and shorten the length to .5; stitch for ¼" to ½" to make the slub. If you have a more modern, computerized machine, program the stitch for a random slub/straight stitch. This is the quickest and easiest way to create the design.

9. After you make test samples and determine that the stitch length, stitch width, and tension are satisfactory, stitch on the first marked vertical line next to the inner border line of each vest piece. Begin and end at the inner border line, stitching to it, but not through it. Leave 3" thread tails. Using the inside toe of your presser foot as a guide, stitch 4 more lines after the marked line. Repeat for all of the remaining vertical and horizontal marked lines. To lock off the threads, pull the thread ends to the wrong side of each piece and knot. Trim the ends to 1".

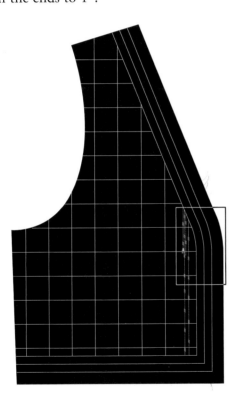

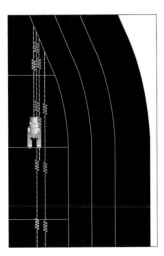

10. Press each piece from the wrong side.

11. Stitch the decorative border stitches determined in step 4 on the marked border lines, selecting from the following methods. If the garment is lined to the edge, embroider each piece separately and sew the pieces together. For a garment with bound edges, sew the shoulder and side seams together before adding borders for a continuous, uninterrupted border around the garment. Start the borders at a seam allowance if the vest has curved front edges. If the garment has a squared front bottom, as in the case of the vest photographed, start the borders at the front corners. This will help make the borders symmetrical on the fronts.

12. Follow the pattern instructions to stitch the fronts to the back at the shoulder seams. Refer to "Easy Vest Lining" on page 109 to assemble and attach the lining, leaving a 1" to 1½" opening at the center back lower edge for inserting the braid ends.

 When attaching the lining, place the lining against the feed dogs. Use the inside edge of the sewing foot to stitch ⅛" away from the border. This makes for a uniform width of fabric between the border and the finished garment edge.

13. Refer to "Mock Piping" on page 103 to stitch the braid to the vest front, neck, and lower edges with invisible thread. Form Sew-As-You-Go loop closures on the vest right front as instructed in "Button Loop Closures" on page 105.

14. Position the buttons on the vest left front to correspond with the loop closure placement, and sew the buttons to the vest.

Linen Bag

Try your hand at free-motion thread painting on a small scale with this enchanting little bag. Once you've mastered the technique, you'll be ready to move on to bigger, more challenging designs.

Finished size: 6" x 8⅝"

MATERIALS

- 8" x 24" piece of medium-weight linen/cotton blend or drapery-weight cotton/acetate blend
- 6½" x 22" piece of lining fabric
- 8" x 24" piece of fusible woven interfacing
- Threads: all-purpose for construction, rayon for flower and leaf embroidery in colors to match embroidery floss, bobbin, gold metallic, invisible monofilament
- Needles: 80/12 universal for invisible thread and garment construction, 75/11 embroidery for single rayon thread, 80/12 topstitching for double rayon thread, 80/12 metallic for metallic thread, tapestry or chenille for hand sewing
- Other materials: darning foot; open-toe appliqué foot; wax-free transfer paper; tracing paper; thread-twisting tool, such as The Spinster described on page 104, for making Spinster braid; 6" to 8" spring hoop for machine embroidery; 3 skeins each of blue and purple embroidery floss; 1 skein each of pink and peach embroidery floss; fine-line black marker; round-tip tool, such as the Stuff-It, for tracing design to fabric; ¾"-diameter gold metallic button

INSTRUCTIONS

1. Prewash or dry-clean the fashion fabric, interfacing, and lining according to the manufacturer's instructions.
2. Following the manufacturer's instructions, fuse the interfacing to the fashion fabric.
3. Using the marker, transfer the design on page 97 to tracing paper.

4. Center the design on the right side of the fashion fabric rectangle, 1" from one end. Pin the paper edge farthest from the rectangle end to the fabric to keep the paper from shifting.

Right side of fabric

1"

5. Slide the transfer paper between the fabric and pattern, placing the chalk side against the fabric. Using a round-tip tool, trace over the pattern design lines to transfer the pattern to the fabric. Remove the pattern.

6. Refer to "Machine Setup and Stitching Techniques" on page 14 to set up the machine for free-motion stitching. Attach the darning foot. Insert the embroidery needle. Thread the needle with the rayon thread color you will use for the flower center. Wind the bobbin with bobbin thread.

7. After you make test samples and determine that the tension is satisfactory, place the fabric end with the pattern traced onto it into the hoop. Place the hoop under the needle. Lower the presser foot, and bring the bobbin thread to the surface.

8. Holding on to the top and bobbin thread, begin stitching the design by outlining the center section of the large flower. Without stopping, stitch just inside the outline stitch. Keep stitching inside each new row until the shape is filled. Stitch in place to lock the threads.

Start here.

Tip

Keep a scrap of fabric hooped to experiment with color combinations before embroidering a new color onto the project.

9. Working from the center of the design out, continue in this manner until all of the flowers and leaves are filled in. To make stems and vines, straight stitch over the design lines three times. Change colors as desired for each motif.

10. When you are finished filling in the design, refer to "Machine Setup and Stitching Techniques" on page 14 to set up the machine for regular sewing. Insert the topstitching needle. Thread the needle with two complementary

colors of rayon thread. Refer to "Sewing with Twin and Triple Needles" on page 16 for threading information. Using a triple straight stitch, stitch on the straight line that borders the embroidery design.

11. Trim the rectangle to 6½" x 22". Leave ½" of fabric on 3 sides of the embroidered end, as shown in the illustration.

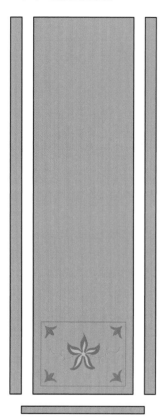

Trim to ½" on 3 sides as shown.

12. Insert the metallic needle into the machine. Thread the needle with the gold metallic thread. Set the stitch for a preprogrammed star design. Randomly stitch stars to the right side of the fashion fabric. If your machine does not have preprogrammed designs, create your own, such as a zigzag stitched in place to make a small, raised dot. Leave thread tails at the end of each star. Pull the thread tails to the bag wrong side and knot the ends together to secure.

13. Refer to "Making Spinster Braid" on page 104 to twist the skeins of peach and pink embroidery floss together. Also braid the skeins of blue and purple floss together. Use 4 total strands for each braid.

14. Return the machine to regular sewing. Insert the universal needle into the machine and attach the open-toe appliqué foot. Using invisible thread in the needle and all-purpose thread in the bobbin, refer to "Threadwork and Couching" on page 72 to zigzag stitch the peach-and-pink braid to the rectangle ¼" above the triple-stitched line that borders the embroidery. Lock off the stitching, and cut off excess braid. Knot the end of the remaining braid so that it will not unravel, and set it aside for later use to embellish the lower edge of the bag.

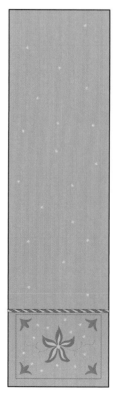

15. With all-purpose thread in the needle and bobbin, stitch the lining to the embroidered fabric, right sides together. Use a ¼" seam allowance. Leave a 4" opening along a long edge and a 1" opening on each side of the embroidered end approximately 5" from the end.

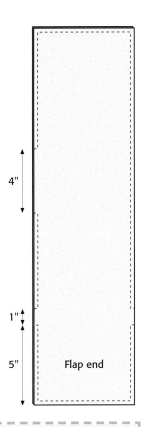

4"

1"

5" Flap end

Tip — When creating openings in the seam allowance, make a right angle turn toward the raw edge and lock the stitches. This encourages the unstitched fabric seam allowance to turn inward after the bag is turned right side out.

16. Trim the corners, and turn the purse right side out through the 4" opening. Press well. Slipstitch the 4" opening closed.

17. Attach the open-toe appliqué foot to the machine. Using invisible thread in the needle and bobbin, refer to "Threadwork and Couching" on page 72 to zigzag stitch the purple-and-blue braid to the edges of the embroidered end. Start by tucking the unknotted end of the braid into a small side

opening; then stitch the braid down on a side of the flap and around the corner. Stop at the center of the flap and backstitch to secure the braid. Using 6" to 8" of braid, make a loop, then butt the remaining braid next to the beginning of the loop. Backstitch a few times and continue to couch around the rest of the flap until you are about 2" from the other 1" opening.

Calculate how much more braid is needed to reach the opening and add about ½" for insertion. Wind a length of thread around the braid and knot the ends at the calculated point so that the braid will not unwind when you cut off the excess braid.

← Thread

Tuck the braid into the opening and continue to couch the remaining braid in place, locking the threads when finished.

18. Return to regular sewing. Refer to "Top-stitching" on page 100 to topstitch the end opposite the embroidered end. Use invisible thread in the needle and bobbin.

19. Lay the rectangle on the ironing board, lining side up. To form the flap, fold the embroidered end over 4½" from the end

along the peach-and-pink braid; press the folded edge, then fold back the flap. Fold the opposite end over 7" to 7½" from the end to form the bag body; press the folded edge. Pin the body sides together and stitch them in place with invisible thread.

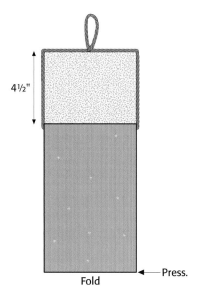

4½"

Fold   ◄— Press.

20. Attach the open-toe appliqué foot to the machine. Using invisible thread in the needle and bobbin, refer to "Threadwork and Couching" on page 72 to zigzag stitch the remaining pink-and-peach braid to the bag-body lower edge, leaving 3" to 4" tails on each end for the tassels. Lock the threads at the beginning and end of the stitching.

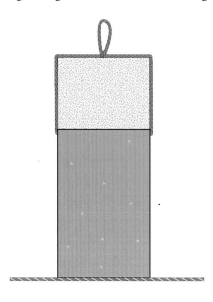

21. From remaining blue-and-purple braid, cut a 4" to 5" piece of braid for the button loop tassel. Make sure to wind a length of thread around the braid and knot the ends at the calculated cutting point so that the braid will not unwind when you cut it. Set it aside.

22. Beginning at the bag lower edge, couch a remaining blue-and-purple braid to the side of the bag, leaving a 3" to 4" tail at the beginning to form a tassel with the pink-and-peach braid. Begin sewing at the bottom of the bag and sew up to and over where the flap braid was inserted, sealing the openings. Leave the remaining braid attached for the shoulder strap. Repeat with a remaining braid on the opposite side.

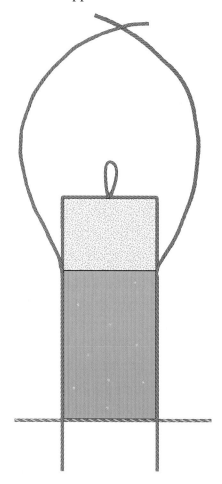

Tie the braids at the bag lower edge together with a single overhand knot. Tie the strap braid ends together in the same manner, leaving 3" to 4" loose.

23. To form the button loop tassel, fold the 4" to 5" blue-and-purple and pink-and-peach braids in half over the button loop.

and wrap for ½". Slide the needle under the wrap and out the opposite end; clip the threads.

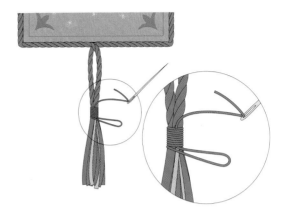

24. Thread a strand of blue or purple floss through a large eye-needle; knot the ends. Lay the knotted ends on the braids and wrap the floss around the braids and over the knotted ends. Begin close to the button loop

25. Unravel the tassel braids and trim the ends to the same length. Fold the flap over the bag body. Stitch the button to the center front of the bag body under the flap loop.

Linen Bag
Embroidery Pattern

Snowflower

This linen jacket was free-motion bobbin stitched with #12 pearl cotton and a design created by my daughter. The jacket edges were finished with pearl cotton Spinster Braid.

Falling Leaves

Appliqué and quilting joined forces for this casual jacket made from wool and silk fabrics. Multicolored wool-crepe leaves were soft-touch machine appliquéd to the wool jacket and secured with a blanket stitch. The wool was then layered with Hobbs Thermore batting and machine quilted with gold thread in a wind-curl design. The jacket was lined and bound with the same wool used for the slacks. All of the appliqué and embroidery work are original designs. Not shown are an embroidered velvet vest and silk blouse.

Stylized Flowers

Take a box of Coats & Clark Rayon Twist, add a challenge to make an embroidered garment, and the end result is this ensemble, created for Coats & Clark in 1997. All of the flowers, leaves, stems, and vines were the result of free-motion stitching. The decorative stitches for the border work were machine-generated. The skirt repeated the border pattern. The jacket, embroidered in a spring hoop, had interfacing added to make the fabric firmer. "Stylized Flowers" received best of show at the 1997 Pennsylvania National Quilt Extravaganza.

Twisted Ribbons

Rayon twist and metallic and rayon threads were used to create this free-motion embroidered wool suit for Coats & Clark in 1998. The twisted ribbons were embroidered and outlined with 2 rows of gold metallic thread. The jacket pieces were then layered with Thermore batting and machine stipple quilted with rayon thread.

Finishing Up

This is a chapter you can refer to again and again as you make the projects throughout the book. It is not filled with inspiring photos, but it is packed with information about finishing your garments so that they will look like they just stepped out of a designer's workroom.

PRESSING

Pressing your garment after construction is every bit as essential as pressing during construction. Seams that do not lie flat are a dead giveaway that the garment is homemade. If you are unable to achieve satisfactory results by using the tools and instructions on page 21, enlist the help of your dry cleaner.

Well-pressed edge finishes are also essential to achieving a professional-looking garment. When pressing the edges of a faced or lined garment, it is important that the lining or facing does not show on the right side of the garment. To do this, roll just a little bit of the right side of the garment toward the inside of the lining when pressing.

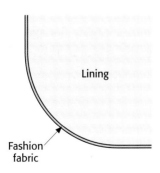

Lining

Fashion fabric

EDGE FINISHES

The instructions in this book refer to one of the three following methods that I use to finish garment edges. Take the time to add one of these touches to your garment, and the professional results will be worth the little time and effort it takes to add them.

Topstitching

Use this technique to keep faced and lined edges where they belong without adding any additional trim.

1. Press the edges thoroughly.
2. Thread the needle with all-purpose thread in a color that matches the fashion fabric. If desired, use two threads and a topstitching needle for more emphasis, or use a single thread of rayon, metallic, or quilting thread with the appropriate needle.
3. Attach an edge-stitching foot to the machine. Place the blade next to the finished garment edge. Move the needle to the left until it is the desired distance from the edge; stitch. I prefer a rather close topstitching line, about ⅛" or less from the edge.

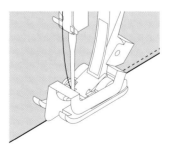

Bias Binding

Continuous single-fold bias binding is a beautiful way to individualize and finish a garment. For a personalized finish, the project instructions in this book call for making your own binding (see "Making Continuous Bias Binding" on page 102), but it also is available in most fabric stores in a limited amount of colors and prints. For examples of custom-created binding, see "Persian Plaid" (page 44) and "Origami Patch Vest" (page 56).

To bind the raw edges of a garment, follow these steps:

1. Stitch along the seam line of the garment raw edges. Trim along the stitched line.

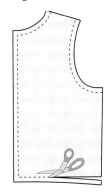

2. Starting on a straight edge, align the binding and garment raw edges, right sides together. Be sure the binding end is cut at a 45° angle.

3. Leaving a 3" length of bias binding unstitched, begin stitching the binding to the edge with a seam allowance the same width as the predetermined finished bias binding. As you approach a corner, miter the binding. To miter the binding, stop stitching a distance equal to your seam allowance from the corner edge; backstitch and remove the garment from the machine.

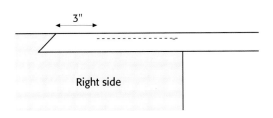

3"

Right side

Fold the binding back on itself, creating a 45°-angle fold.

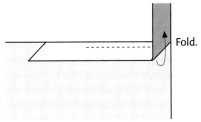

Fold.

Fold the binding down so that the raw edges are even with the second edge, and the fold is even with the first edge. Pin in place.

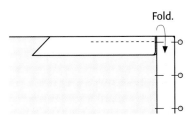

Fold.

Beginning at the fold, resume stitching. Backstitch as you start. Repeat for all of the corners.

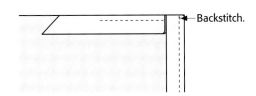

Backstitch.

4. Continue stitching the binding to the garment until you are 6" to 8" from the starting point. Cut the binding end so it overlaps the beginning by at least 3". Lay the end of the strip (B) over the beginning of the strip (A). Make sure both ends are lying flat against the garment. Mark the edges of B where it meets A. Connect the marks to make a diagonal line on B.

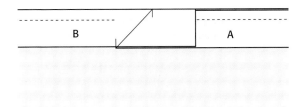

B   A

Making Continuous Bias Binding

With this method, you can make a long, continuous strip of bias binding from a square of fabric.

1. Determine the finished width of the binding. Typically, the finished binding is ¼", ⅜", or ½" wide. Multiply the finished width by 4 and add ⅜" to ¼", depending on how thick the edge to be bound is. For example, if you want a ⅜"-wide finished binding, you would need to cut the bias strips 1⅝" wide (⅜" x 4 = 1²⁄₈ + ⅛ = 1³⁄₈ = 1⅝"). To calculate how much binding is needed, measure along the edges where the binding will be stitched. Multiply that number by the binding width, and then find the square root. Round off this number to the next highest even number. The number is the size of the square to cut. For example, if you need 180" of 1¾"-wide binding, you will need an 18" square of fabric (180" x 1¾" = 315". The square root of 315 is 17.7).

2. From the fabric indicated in the instructions, cut the square of fabric the size determined. Cut the square in half on the diagonal.

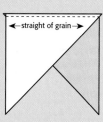

Cut.

3. With the right sides together, stitch the halves together as shown. Using a ¼" seam allowance, sew along the straight-grain edges. Press the seam allowance open.

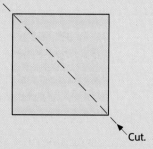

←straight of grain→

4. On the right side of the fabric, make a 6" cut the width of the bias binding. This will be the start of the binding.

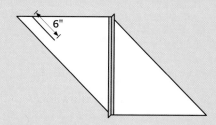

6"

5. With right sides together, bring the remaining 2 straight edges together as shown, to form a tube. Stitch them together with a ¼" seam. Press the seam open. There will be a small amount of fabric left at the end of the seam.

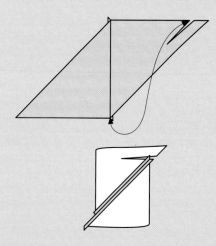

6. Slip a small cutting board inside the tube and use your rotary cutter and ruler to cut the bias strip the predetermined width.

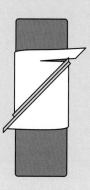

5. Draw a second line ½" away from the first line. Cut along the second line.

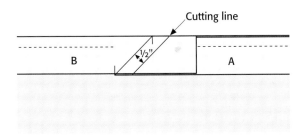

6. With right sides together, stitch the ends together with a ¼" seam allowance.

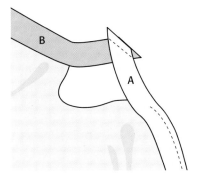

7. Finish stitching the binding to the edge.
8. Fold the binding over the raw edges to the inside of the garment, covering the machine stitching. Tuck under the excess binding and hand stitch the binding in place along the fold.

Mock Piping

Mock piping is actually a braided trim that is stitched to the finished edges of a garment. For examples, see "Burgundy Twist" (page 65) and "Pintuck Surprise" (page 63). Trim purchased from the fabric store can be used, but making your own provides you with endless options for customizing the finished look. Select pearl cotton, embroidery floss, yarn, or any other type of thread or cord, and twist your own braid together. Sound daunting? Don't let it be. The Spinster, a thread-twisting tool, makes the task easy. Refer to "Making Spinster Braid" on page 104 to make your own twisted creations.

To apply mock piping, follow these steps:

1. Refer to "Easy Vest Lining" on page 109 to line the vest, leaving a 1" to 1½" openings in the seam allowance of the garment at the center back neck for purchased braid. This opening allows the ends of the braid to be hidden in the seam allowance and secured during the stitching process. For Spinster braid, I have found that I can make only 1½ yards of braid by myself, so I leave openings in the center back neckline and the hemline for insertion on garments that are lined to the edge. This also requires making 2 braids to cover the length of the outer edges. If your garment is faced, leave insertion openings at the same place.

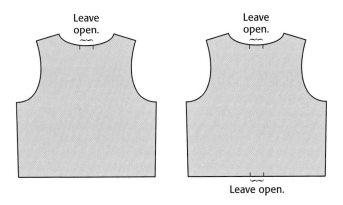

For purchased braid   For spinster braid

Making Spinster Braid

The Spinster is a must-have tool for making your own customized braids. As a general rule of thumb, you need about three yards of some type of thread, cord, or yarn to make a yard of finished braid. Try three to four strands of pearl cotton for a nice finished braid, or embroidery floss for a beautiful, soft braid. Even 1"-wide bias-edge silk ribbon makes a great braid. For a glitzy look, combine ribbon or pearl cotton with metallic braids. The options are endless!

To make a braid for edge finishing with The Spinster, follow these steps:

1. Cut 3 lengths, 3 yards each, of the desired thread(s). Tie the ends together in an overhand knot.
2. Attach an end of the thread group to a stationary object. (I put a paper clip into a C clamp that is attached to my worktable, then loop an end in the paper clip.) Place the other end into the cup hook on The Spinster tool. Walk away from the stationary object until the threads are taut. Wind the tool until the strands are twisted into a cord and the handle is harder to turn.

3. Holding the thread ends attached to The Spinster, unhook the threads from the tool and set the tool aside. Pinch the twisted threads at the halfway point. Bring the 2 ends together and allow the braids to twist on each other to create a finished braid.

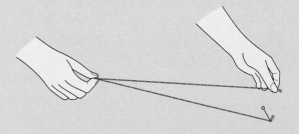

4. Tie the ends together.

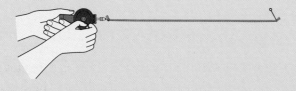

To achieve a candy cane effect, cut three strands of threads in one color and three strands in another color. Tie the ends of one color strand together with an overhand knot. Thread one end of the other color through the loop of the first color, then tie the strands of the second color together in an overhand knot. Use The Spinster to make the braid.

2. Thread the machine with invisible monofilament thread in the needle and bobbin. Place the appliqué foot on the machine. Set the machine for a zigzag stitch with a width wide enough that a swing of the needle just catches the fabric and the other swing lands in the middle of the braid. Set the stitch length at about 2.5.

3. Starting at an opening, place the garment edge under the center of the appliqué foot. Place the braid next to the garment edge, leaving 1" loose to tuck in later.

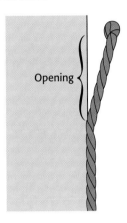

Opening

Stitch the braid to the garment. If you miss a spot, backstitch and go over it again. If you are using Spinster braid, start with the finished end.

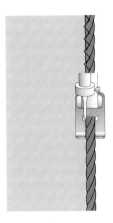

When you are about 2" from the next opening, stop with the needle in the fabric. Calculate the amount of braid needed to reach the opening plus 1" for tucking into the opening. With a hand-sewing needle and thread, tie off the braid at the determined point and cut away the excess braid.

Thread

Continue to attach the braid. When you reach the opening, tuck the end of the stitched braid and approximately 1" of a new braid end into the opening so that they cross over each other.

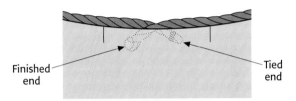

Finished end

Tied end

4. Stitch across the opening, attaching both braids to the garment. Continue stitching the new braid to the garment. To finish off, use the same procedure to cross the ends over at the beginning opening. Backstitch to lock off.

BUTTON LOOP CLOSURES

Buttons and buttonholes are probably the most common closure, but it is easy to vary the standard opening with some simple techniques for making button loops. Try either of the Sew-As-You-Go button loop variations when using the mock piping method (see page 103) to trim your garment. Version 1 produces a flat, invisible opening, while Version 2 creates a visible loop. For examples of Version 1, see "Orchid Sky" (page 32) and "It's Always Greener" (page 73). A photo of a garment with Version 2 button loops is shown on page 110.

Fabric button loops are yet another way to

personalize your garment's closures. Simple-to-make fabric strips are formed into loops and stitched to the garment front before the facing or lining is added. For an example, see "Calla Lilies" (page 83).

Sew-As-You-Go Button Loops

Version 1

1. Before you stitch the braid to the garment, mark where the buttons are to be stitched on the left vest front. Place a pin at the corr-esponding edge of the right front piece. Center the buttons over each pin and place another pin approximately ⅛" on each side of the button. Remove the pin under the button.

NOTE: MAKE A MOCK LOOP USING THE PIN SPAC-ING TO BE SURE THE LOOP IS LARGE ENOUGH FOR THE BUTTON TO EASILY SLIDE THROUGH THE LOOP.

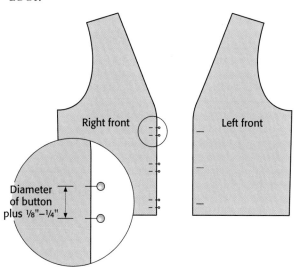

2. Stitch the braid to the garment, following the instructions in "Mock Piping" on page 103. When you reach the first pin marking the button opening, backstitch to reinforce the opening, and reset the machine for a straight stitch. Stitch along the fabric edge until you

reach the next pin. Return to a zigzag stitch and take 2 or 3 stitches. Then back-stitch to reinforce the loop. Continue to attach the braid to the edge until you reach the next pin. Repeat to leave the braid unstitched between the pins for

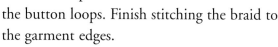

the button loops. Finish stitching the braid to the garment edges.

Version 2

1. Before you stitch the braid to the garment, determine where the buttons are to be stitched on the left front piece, and place a straight pin at the corresponding edge of the right front piece.

2. Stitch the braid to the garment, follow-ing the instructions in "Mock Piping" on page 103. When you come to a pin, stop stitching, leaving the needle in the fabric. Measure out between 2" and 3" of braid, depending on the size of the button, and insert a pin into the braid. Make a test sample ahead of time

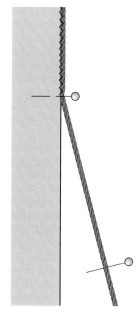

to determine the exact amount of braid needed to form the loop appropriate for the button.

3. Cross the braid over itself to form a loop and insert the pinned braid portion at the point where you stopped stitching. Begin stitching again, stitching over the crossed braid.

4. Repeat steps 2 and 3 until all of the button loops are formed and the braid is stitched to the edge.

Fabric Button Loops

1. After the garment is embellished, but before the lining or front facings are added, cut a 1"-wide bias strips from the fashion fabric. Press the strip in half lengthwise, wrong sides together.

Turn the raw edges in to meet the folded edge; press.

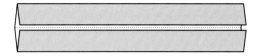

Pin the new outer folded edges together and stitch along the folds.

2. To determine the lengths to cut the strip, wrap the strip around the button you will be using, allowing enough room to pass the button through. Add an additional 1¼" to that length for the seam allowance. Cut a strip the length determined for each button.

3. Determine where the buttons are to be stitched on the left front piece, and place a straight pin at the corresponding edge of the right front piece. Place the loop raw edges side by side at the pin mark to form a loop, aligning them with the garment raw edge. Pin the ends in place. It does not matter whether the seamed edges or folded edges are placed on the outside or inside of the loop. Baste the ends in place ½" from the garment edge.

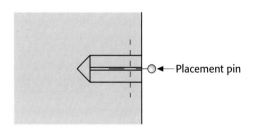

4. Add the facing or lining as instructed.

SEAM FINISHES

Look inside any piece of designer clothing and you will undoubtedly find exquisitely finished seams—not a raw edge in sight. Follow their lead and never have a thread out of place.

French Seam

French seams are an efficient way to encase the seam allowances of lightweight fabric that can be seen through or fabrics that ravel. To make a French seam, follow these steps:

1. With *wrong* sides together, stitch ¼" from the edge. Press the seam allowance to one side.

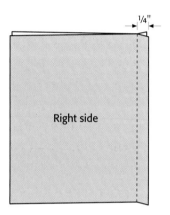

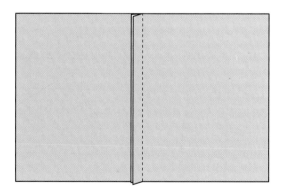

2. Turn the garment pieces so that they are right sides together, and press the seams flat. Stitch ⅜" from the folded edge.

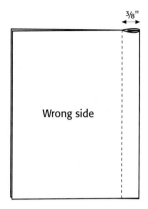

Flat-Felled Seam

Because this seam is enclosed and then stitched down, reversible garments are good candidates for flat-felled seams. To stitch a flat-felled seam, follow these steps:

1. Stitch the garment seams together as usual. Press the seams open, then trim the inner seam allowance to ¼".

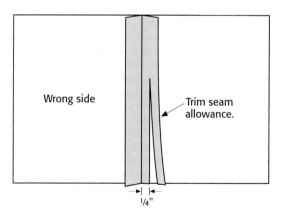

2. Press the outer seam allowance over the inner seam allowance.

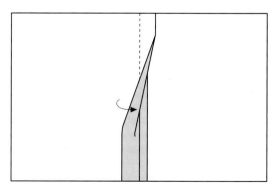

3. Fold under the seam allowance raw edge to meet the original seam. Press. Stitch close to the folded edge. If desired, stitch close to the original seam.

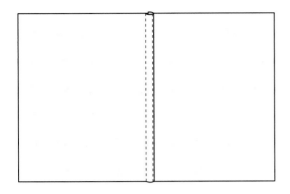

 If you are finishing a quilted garment with flat-felled seams, trim some of the batting in the seam allowances to lessen the bulk.

Bias-Bound Seam

Bias binding is yet another way to finish seams. It can be done on the inside of a garment or on the outside. Try using a contrast fabric for accent.

1. Trim the seam allowances to ¼".
2. Prepare the binding strip as directed in "Making Continuous Bias Binding" on page 102, cutting 1¼"-wide strips. (That measurement was derived by multiplying the seam width by 4 and adding ¼" for seam bulk.)
3. Align a raw edge of the binding with the trimmed seam edge and stitch it to the seam allowance with a ¼" seam. Wrap the binding over the seam allowance layers and tuck under

the raw edge ¼". Stitch the folded edge to the garment by hand.

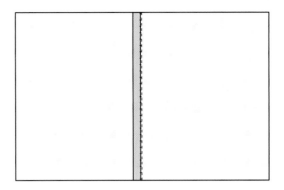

EASY VEST LINING

Eliminate garment facings by using this easy lined-to-the-edge method.

1. Stitch the front and back lining pieces together at the shoulder seams. Press the seams open. Press the shoulder seams of the vest fashion fabric open.
2. Pin the vest and lining right sides together at the armhole, neckline, and center front edges. Match the shoulder seams.
3. Stitch around the armhole openings. Beginning 3" from a front-piece lower edge, stitch the fronts together. End stitching at the center back neckline. Repeat for the remaining front edge. Trim the seams to ¼" and clip the curves.

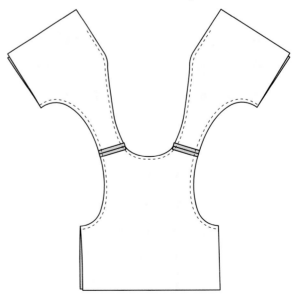

4. Turn the vest right side out by reaching into the vest back and grabbing the bottom of the vest fronts. Pull the fronts through the shoulder and out the back opening.

5. Matching the underarm seams, pin the lining and vest side seams right sides together. Stitch the seam, beginning at the back and ending at the front. Press the seam open and clip seam allowance if necessary.

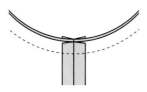

6. Place the vest, right side out, on a flat surface. Pick up the unstitched edge of the vest lining and roll it over the vest body to the back of

the vest to meet the bottom edge of the vest back fashion fabric. With right sides together, pin the vest and lining edges.

7. Stitch edges together, leaving a 4" or 5" opening in the center back to turn the vest right side out. Stitch right angles at the opening to facilitate turning.

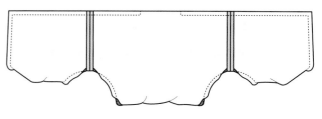

8. Clip corners and curves; then trim seam allowances to ¼". Turn garment right side out.

9. Press all edges and edge stitch to finish.

Version 2 button loop closures are used in this garment, "Desert Stripes."

Resources

Fabrics

Artemis Hand-Dyed Silk Ribbons, 179 High Street, South Portland, ME 04106
www.artemisinc.com

Thai Silks, 252 State Street, Los Altos, CA 94022
800-722-7455 outside California
800-221-7455 in California

Publications

Threads, The Taunton Press, 63 S. Main St., PO Box 5507, Newtown, CT 06470-9875
800-888-8286
www.threadsmagazine.com

Sew News, PO Box 56907, Boulder, CO 80322
800-289-6397
www.sewnews.com

Threads

The Thread Shed, PO Box 898, Horseshoe, NC 28742

Web of Thread, 1410 Broadway, Paducah, KY 42003
800-955-8185
www.webofthread.com

Tools

Clotilde Inc., PO Box 3000, Louisiana, MO 63353-3000, 800-824-4537
www.clotilde.com

Nancy's Notions, PO Box 683, Beaver Dam, WI 53916-0683
800-833-0690
www.nancysnotions.com

Classes and Lectures

For a copy of Patricia Nelson's teaching schedule, send a stamped, self-addressed envelope to Patricia Nelson, 119 Edward Street, Athens, PA, 18810. Her email address is david.nelson@cyber-quest.com

Bibliography

Adachi, Fumie, trans. *Japanese Design Motifs: 4260 Illustrations of Japanese Crests.* New York: Dover Publications, 1972.

Editors of Cy DeCosse, Inc. *The Perfect Fit.* Minnetonka, Minn.: Cy DeCosse, Inc.,1987.

Farro, Rita. *Life Is Not a Dress Size: Rita Farro's Guide to Attitude, Style and a New You.* Radnor, Pa: Chilton Book Co., 1996.

Fraga, Mack. *Ready to Use Snowflake Designs.* Mineola, N.Y.: Dover Publications, 1991.

Grafton, Carol Belanger. *1,001 Floral Motifs and Ornaments for Artists and Craftspeople.* Mineola, N.Y.: Dover Publications, 1987.

Hazen, Gale Grigg. *Fantastic Fit for Every Body: How to Alter Patterns to Flatter Any Body.* Emmaus, Pa: Rodale Press, 1998.

Orban-Szontagh, Madeleine. *Traditional Floral Designs and Motifs for Artists and Craftspeople.* Mineola, NY: Dover Publications, 1989.

Rasband, Judith. *Fabulous Fit.* New York: Fairchild Publications, 1994.

About the Author

Like many of her fellow quilters, Patricia started sewing when she was very young. Her first projects were doll clothes made with scraps from her mother's sewing box. She sewed through high school, and then went on to nursing school, where she became a registered nurse. She didn't start sewing again until she married and bought her first sewing machine. She has moved quite a bit and each move has brought a new sewing experience for her.

Patricia is a machine-oriented sewer and has been teaching machine-related sewing classes for over twenty years. She loves the challenge of converting traditional handwork to machine. In 1977, she became very absorbed in machine embroidery and appliqué and gradually expanded into a wide array of machine techniques. In the last couple of years, she has primarily focused on creating wearable quilted garments. She continues to experiment with new machine techniques and enjoys passing them on to students.

Patricia has won numerous ribbons for her wearables, including Best of Show at the AQS Fashion Show, the International Quilt Show in Houston, the Pennsylvania National Quilt Extravaganza, and the Hoffman Challenge. She has also been invited to participate in the Fairfield Fashion Show twice, and her garments have traveled all over the United States and Vienna, Austria. They have also traveled to Australia with Hobb's Bonded Fibers.

Patricia has been published by *Country Crafts, Threads,* and *American Quilter.*